11 95

VGM Opportunities Series

D0167280

OPPORTUNITIES IN
HOME ECONOMICS
CAREERS

Rhea Shields, Ph.D.
Anna K. Williams

Revised Edition

Foreword by
Karen E. Craig
Dean, College of Human Resources and Family Sciences
University of Nebraska-Lincoln

VGM Career Horizons
NTC/Contemporary Publishing Group

Library of Congress Cataloging-in-Publication Data

Shields, Rhea.
   Opportunities in home economics careers / Rhea Shields, Anna K.
Williams.—Rev. ed. / revised by Julie Rigby.
      p.   cm. — (VGM opportunities series)
   ISBN 0-658-00201-5 (cloth) — ISBN 0-658-00202-3 (paperback)
      1. Home economics—Vocational guidance—United States.   I. Williams,
Anna K.   II. Rigby, Julie.   III. Title.   IV. Series.

TX164 .S55   2000
640'.023'73—dc21   99-53373
                                                               CIP

Cover photograph: © PhotoDisc, Inc.

Published by VGM Career Horizons
A division of NTC/Contemporary Publishing Group, Inc.
4255 West Touhy Avenue, Lincolnwood (Chicago), Illinois 60712-1975 U.S.A.
Printed in the United States of America
International Standard Book Number: 0-658-00201-5 (cloth)
                                        0-658-00202-3 (paper)

00   01   02   03   04   05   LB   15   14   13   12   11   10   9   8   7   6   5   4   3   2   1

CONTENTS

American Home Economics Association. Creed of
home economics. The expansion of the field. Updating
the creed. A new name, a continuing emphasis. Suggested
additional reading.

Training in interior design. Residential and commercial
design. Skills required. Professional organizations. Job
outlook. Profile: interior designer. Profile: freelance interior
decorator. Suggested additional reading.

A role in the heart of a company. What do home economists
do? Professional organizations. Salary. Profile: consumer
affairs professional. Profile: test kitchen professional.
Suggested additional reading.

ABOUT THE AUTHORS

Dr. Rhea Shields has enjoyed a long and rewarding career in home economics. Rhea has been the director of home economics for four different companies: Carrollton Manufacturing, Deepfreeze Appliances, Arvin Industries, and Robertshaw Controls. She received her Ph.D. in home management and agricultural economics from Michigan State University in 1966. Rhea was an assistant professor of home economics for ten years at Western Illinois University. She then served as a professor and chairperson of the home economics department at Chicago State University from 1968 to 1984. In 1984, Rhea was named Outstanding Home Economist by the Illinois Home Economics Association. Dr. Shields is currently a home economics consultant residing in Palos Heights, Illinois.

Anna K. Williams has been actively involved with home economics for more than forty years. She received her B.S. in home economics from Purdue University. She later earned an M.A. in social science from the University of Chicago and an M.A. in economics from Indiana University.

Anna K. has been a home economics teacher, a cooperative extension agent at Purdue University, and a specialist in home management and family economics at Purdue. She also has served as legislative chairperson for the Indiana Home Economics Association. She has served as a director on the boards of several nonprofit organizations. Anna K. currently resides in Crown Point, Indiana, and she works for the Consumer Credit Counseling Service of Northwest Indiana.

FOREWORD

Choosing one's life work in contemporary society is very complex. Expectations for fulfillment in work and personal lives are changing. *Opportunities in Home Economics Careers* provides insight into the role of home economics and family and consumer sciences professionals in contemporary society. As a mission-oriented profession, home economics careers change as society changes. The same set of skills, relative to nutrition, child development, family relationships, clothing, and the near environment, serve as the basis for employment in business, public and private agency settings, education, and the volunteer sector. That flexibility allows professionals to use their personal talents in many ways.

This book identifies a variety of careers that evolve from application of science to the arts, physical and social sciences, and the humanities as they relate to daily living in a complex world. No matter what your strengths or interests, there may be a career in your future that evolves from the heritage of home economics. In the pages that follow, you will see many options with roots in the application of science to daily problems, using a home economics perspective.

As you explore career ideas in this book, look for the ideal match of your interests, skills, attitudes, and personal goals as they relate to a career. Making that perfect match will serve you and society well. It will help you be the best that you can be!

Karen E. Craig
Dean, College of Human Resources and Family Sciences
University of Nebraska–Lincoln

ACKNOWLEDGMENTS

The authors gratefully acknowledge Marie Vosicky for her contribution to Chapter 9 of this book.

CHAPTER 1

AN INTRODUCTION TO HOME ECONOMICS

"Home economics" conjures up for most people the image of junior high school girls either in cooking class or working on sewing projects, while the boys are down the hall doing shop and auto maintenance. In fact, that outdated image is far from the truth! Modern home economics is taught to both male and female students, often beginning in elementary school and continuing through high school. From there, many women and men go on to receive undergraduate and even advanced degrees in home economics.

The history of home economics runs parallel to the history of women's education. Two hundred years ago, those women who were fortunate enough to receive an education often did so in schools that imparted both academic and practical studies. Over the centuries, household tasks and the care of young children had come to be seen as the proper role for women, while men dedicated their energies to hunting, fishing, or establishing agriculture, trade, and markets. Thus, young women were trained in the domestic arts, as well as in reading and writing. Some of the first books written on "domestic economy," by Catherine Beecher, are seen as the real beginnings of the home economics movement. Nevertheless, education in other fields, such as law, medicine, and theology, which were the main academic subjects of the era, was largely closed to women.

In the years leading up to the Civil War in the United States, there was a concerted effort to apply new knowledge to the everyday problems of farmers and working people. In 1862, President Lincoln signed the Morrill Land Grant Act. This very popular act provided subsidies for state universities, with the stipulation that there be instruction in agriculture, mechanical arts, and military training. These universities, serving the needs of the resident population, became a natural home for the newly developing discipline of home economics.

AMERICAN HOME ECONOMICS ASSOCIATION

The American Home Economics Association was formed in 1909 and grew out of a series of meetings known as the Lake Placid Conferences. At these conferences, it was agreed that the term "home economics" be used rather than terms such as "domestic science" or "household arts."

One of the most influential figures in home economics was Ellen S. Richards. Richards was the first chairperson of the Lake Placid Conferences, and she guided the group through the next ten meetings. She also served as the first president of the American Home Economics Association. This remarkable woman graduated from Vassar in 1870 and then convinced the authorities at the Massachusetts Institute of Technology to admit her as a special student in chemistry. She was the first female to graduate from MIT; later she became MIT's first female professor. Richards advocated for consumer education, child protection, nutrition, industrial safety, public health, and women's rights. She also is credited by historians as originating the concept of ecology.

CREED OF HOME ECONOMICS

Richards created a creed of home economics, stating that it stands for the following:

- the ideal home life for today unhampered by the traditions of the past
- the utilization of all the resources of modern science to improve the home life
- the freedom of the home from the dominance of things and their due subordination to ideals
- the simplicity in material surroundings that will most free the spirit for the more important and permanent interests of the home and society

THE EXPANSION OF THE FIELD

The contribution of home economists during the first World War brought to them enough public regard that the Smith Hughes Act of 1917 specifically named home economics as a field for federally subsidized teacher training.

The Smith Hughes Act provided federal appropriations and encouraged states to provide for vocational education. According to the Smith Hughes Act, in order for federal money to be expended, the state or local community or both must provide facilities and funding. This influx of money for secondary education brought a large expansion in both the quantity and quality of home economics courses in most communities.

The Smith Lever Act of 1914 brought home economics to rural people through the Cooperative Extension Service. It brought about the cooperation of federal, state, and local appropriating bodies for specific adult and out-of-school education programs in approximately three thousand counties in the United States. These two acts—Smith Hughes and Smith Lever—have been responsible for a large part of the growth of the home economics profession by providing funding and setting standards.

From World War I until the early 1960s, vocational education developed with several acts of Congress providing for various programs for different categories of people. In the late sixties, the public became aware of the need for coordinating employment programs with vocational education. This brought about changes. The 1968 amendments reflect a general trend in shifting funding from occupational categories to program categories. In home economics there is increased activity in training for employment in related (away from home) occupations. Consumer and homemaking education is still a line item in the federal budget.

UPDATING THE CREED

Over the years there have been attempts to update the creed developed by Ellen Swallow Richards. Currently the bylaws of the Home Economics Association say that a home economist is one who holds a bachelor's degree or an advanced degree with a major in home economics or a specialized area of home economics from an accredited college or university in the United States or Canada.

On its fiftieth anniversary in 1959, the American Home Economics Association published a statement of philosophy and objectives called "New Directions." In this statement home economics is defined as the field of knowledge and service primarily concerned with strengthening family life through the following:

- educating the individual through family living
- improving the goods and services used by families
- conducting research on the changing needs of individuals and the means of satisfying these needs
- furthering community, national, and world conditions favorable to family living

A NEW NAME, A CONTINUING EMPHASIS

Changes in the profession of home economics are responses to changes in the American family and society. Over the years, professionals belonging to the American Home Economics Association found themselves engaged in a more broadly defined discipline. At a conference in 1993 in Scottsdale, Arizona, more than one hundred professionals representing twenty-one related professional organizations gathered to discuss the changing face of home economics. It was decided at that time that the AHEA's name should be changed to reflect the true nature of what the profession had become. The name decided upon was The American Association of Family and Consumer Sciences.

The American Association of Family and Consumer Sciences (AAFCS) continues to hold to the values expressed by Ellen Richards, who worked to apply scientific and management principles to the family and household.

The AAFCS sees its mission as working toward the optimal well-being of families and individuals by:

- empowering members to act on continuing and emerging concerns
- focusing the expertise of members for action on critical issues
- assuming leadership among organizations with mutual purposes

In the course of defining its roles and mission, the AAFCS also has articulated what it considers its core values:

- families as the fundamental social unit
- research as a base for new and expanding knowledge
- innovation, creativity, and application of research to solve problems of individuals and families

- holistic, interdisciplinary, integrative, and preventive perspectives in addressing the issues of individuals and families as consumers
- diversity, equality, and human rights
- both global and community perspectives when addressing issues of individuals and families as consumers
- reciprocal relationships between people and their environments, which affect the quality of their lives
- the forging of partnerships and collaborations with others who share our values and purposes
- lifelong learning
- a healthy global environment that positively impacts the human condition
- the profession as a force in shaping public policy

At the start of a new century, the profession of home economics has come to embrace far more than the traditional domestic roles assigned to women. It is a field that encompasses many radical changes affecting the human population, from information technology, to genetically engineered foods, to new theories and practices in social welfare. As such, it is a profession that attracts innovative and ambitious people, both male and female.

SUGGESTED ADDITIONAL READING

Stage, Sarah and Virginia B. Vincenti, editors. *Rethinking Home Economics: Women and the History of a Profession.* Ithaca, NY: Cornell University Press, 1997.

CHAPTER 2

INTERIOR DESIGN: HABITATS FOR LIVING AND WORKING

The homes we live in and the offices in which we work are more than merely four walls and a roof. We also require that the environments we inhabit be comfortable, pleasing to the eye, and conducive to productivity. Increasingly, individuals, families, and businesses turn to the expertise of the professional interior designer to create the most satisfying living and working environments.

According to the *Occupational Outlook Handbook* from the U.S. Department of Labor:

> *Interior designers* plan the space and furnish the interiors of private homes, public buildings, and commercial establishments, such as offices, restaurants, hospitals, hotels, and theaters. They also may plan additions and renovations. With a client's tastes, needs, and budget in mind, they develop designs and prepare working drawings and specifications for interior construction, furnishings, lighting, and finishes. Increasingly, designers use computers to plan layouts that can be changed easily to include ideas received

from the client. They also design lighting and architectural details such as crown molding, coordinate colors, and select furniture, floor coverings, and curtains. Interior designers must design space in accordance with Federal, State, and local laws, including building codes. Increasingly, they plan spaces that meet accessibility standards for the disabled and elderly.

TRAINING IN INTERIOR DESIGN

Most colleges and universities granting degrees in home economics include departments of related art and interior design. Many community colleges and art schools also offer classes in interior design. University training generally includes basic arts and sciences and specialized courses such as drawing techniques, textiles, lighting, art history, and period furniture. One advantage of studying interior design within the framework of a home economics degree is the opportunity to correlate courses in household equipment, family living, and consumer economics with the specialized design program. Home economics education is usually a major program in these universities, and thus courses are available in such areas as demonstration techniques and the preparation of illustrative material.

At a university it is possible to "tailor make" an education aimed at a specialized career. It is also possible to earn a more generalized degree that will serve as a background for a variety of job opportunities. One also can prepare for a career in interior design in an art school or a school of architecture. Diplomas and associate degrees are available in a variety of technical schools and community colleges.

While course work is always in one's best interests, there is also nothing like old-fashioned on-the-job experience for really giving you a feel for interior design as a career. Part-time positions in retail stores are available to college students and sometimes high school students. These experiences can be combined with technical courses to work one's way up the career ladder. It is possible to go from associate degrees to graduate degrees and from beginning jobs to top positions in well-known design firms.

RESIDENTIAL AND COMMERCIAL DESIGN

Positions are usually more specialized in either residential or commercial work. Commercial interior designers work with restaurants, hotels, office complexes, nursing homes, schools, and shopping centers. The line between commercial and residential design is not hard and fast. For example, apartment complexes and retirement homes could be classified as either residential or commercial. Some designers are employed by manufacturers for the purpose of promoting their products; others are employed to write and edit magazine articles or write syndicated columns.

Interior designers, after consultation with their clients, draw plans to scale, sketch wallpaper samples and other illustrations, and present their ideas to their clients, first in a rough draft and then in more refined detail. Designers also calculate costs, including materials and labor. After selling their ideas, they may purchase or supervise the purchase of materials, oversee construction, and follow through on installation. The job is not complete until the customer is satisfied.

SKILLS REQUIRED

In order to succeed in interior design you must be able to apply art principles to interior spaces. Designers need to know the uses of furnishings and equipment, as well as the space itself so that the results will be both practical and efficient. Competence in mathematics also is called for, as one must accurately determine scale drawings, perform measurements involved in construction, and estimate costs. The designer must be able to communicate and sell ideas to clients. The profession requires an appreciation for history and craftsmanship, as well as a sense of the social and economic influences of the present.

In the last two decades, a changing workforce as well as the explosion in the use of home computers has greatly increased the need for interior designers. Families with both spouses employed have more money and less time to spend on do-it-yourself interior projects. A home economics background uniquely qualifies the provider of specialized services to understand the needs of the customers or clients.

PROFESSIONAL ORGANIZATIONS

Interior design is the only design field subject to government regulation. In 1997, twenty-two states required licensing for interior designers. Because licensing is not mandatory in all states, membership in a professional organization is a recognized mark of qualification for interior designers. Membership usually requires three or four years of postsecondary education in design, at least two years of practical experience, and completion of the National Council for Interior Design qualification exam.

The following are professional organizations in the field of interior design:

American Society for Interior Designers
608 Massachusetts Avenue NW
Washington, DC 20002-6006
www.asid.org

The Foundation for Interior Design Education Research
60 Monroe Center NW
Grand Rapids, MI 49503
www.fider.org

Industrial Designers Society of America
1142-E Walker Road
Great Falls, VA 22066
www.idsa.org

JOB OUTLOOK

Prospects for the increasing numbers of people employed in interior design are excellent, with starting salaries between

$18,000 and $20,000. Salaries after five years' experience average from $30,000 to $37,000.

Future interior designers face stiff competition, as this is a field that attracts many talented, creative people. However, opportunities for interior designers are expected to be abundant through the year 2006.

PROFILE: INTERIOR DESIGNER

For Gwen, a senior at a major university, the prospect of being selected for an interior design position by a manufacturer of mobile homes was exciting. She became the first home economist the five-year-old corporation employed.

The position was an excellent opportunity to put into practice her skill in designing built-in furnishings and selecting appropriate pieces to complete compact homes. The president of the company had risked a good deal of his own money in establishing the enterprise. He was a graduate of her university and noticed her creative efforts and thorough work. After only one year she was invited to accompany the corporation's group that attended a trade show where they exhibited for the first time. Changes in their product that had resulted from Gwen's work were admired by competitors, and she came back to her task most encouraged. She was soon rewarded with a substantial raise in salary.

Gwen took the initiative in discussing the materials that might be substituted in mobile home interiors with engineers and other workers in the plant. She enrolled in an engineering design course at a nearby college in order to become more competent in her efforts. After the Home Economics Association state meeting, she brought to the vice president of her division the idea of contacting high schools about incorporating the use of a mobile home into the family living curriculum. The idea became a profitable venture for the corporation.

Gwen's father had become interested in mobile home corporations as an investment opportunity and purchased a sizable number of shares of stock. She herself had become a small investor in her company.

Even when the company suffered some financial setbacks, which reflected industrywide problems, Gwen remained in a good position with the company. Indeed, during the downturns, when the price of the corporation's stock was low, both Gwen and her father were able to purchase more shares.

The last five years have seen a dramatic increase in the value of their investment because business has been excellent in the mobile home industry. Now Gwen is a vice president herself and has two home economists and the public relations department working under her direction. Along the way, she completed a master's in business administration and is now a part of the top management of the corporation.

Over the years, the managers at Gwen's company have received healthy bonuses. For example, one year Gwen received a $40,000 bonus. When added to her salary of $45,000 and her dividends on the stock in the company,

Gwen was earning in the top income tax bracket before she reached age thirty-nine.

PROFILE: FREELANCE INTERIOR DECORATOR

Andrew is a freelance home economist specializing in interior design. When Andrew receives a request for assistance, he sets up an appointment in the home of his client. At this initial meeting, Andrew and his new client can come to a mutual understanding as to the goals for the project.

In one typical case, Andrew met his client, Mary Adams, for the first interview. Mary explained that she wanted to completely redo the public rooms—living room, dining room, family room, and hall. Andrew asked the following questions: "Do you use the dining room daily or weekly? How many people are in your family? What are the ages of the children? What are their hobbies? What are your favorite colors? Describe your lifestyle. What is your budget? What pieces of furniture do you plan to replace?"

Once Andrew and Mary agreed that Andrew would proceed with the project, he took measurements for each room and for the furniture that was to be kept. Before the second visit Andrew had drawn the rooms to scale on graph paper, including the furniture. He also prepared three options of arrangements, as well as some three-dimensional sketches in color. He further collected samples of wallpaper, curtains, and carpet.

During the second interview, Andrew asked the client to mentally and verbally rehearse the family's activities within the scaled drawings. He left the samples and drawings with the client for a family conference.

On the third visit to the client's home, Andrew and Mary decided on the items in the final selection, making sure that the colors in the various rooms were coordinated and that the specific colors flowed easily from room to room.

Andrew ordered draperies, curtains, and carpets within the budget and specified the date of delivery. He also shopped for furniture and pictures. He then proceeded to order wallpaper and paint.

Andrew invites clients to accompany him on the final shopping trip for furniture and accessories. He assumes the responsibility for being present at the time of delivery of furniture, carpeting, and draperies. He also assumes the responsibility of the workers who install carpets, paint walls, and apply wallpaper.

Once the design specifications have been carried out, Andrew makes a final visit for evaluation and adjustments. It is important to Andrew that the client is pleased because future contracts depend on a good reputation.

During the initial interview with Mary, Andrew mentally estimated the amount of time the job would require and the amount of money he would make as commission on the furniture, draperies, carpeting, painting, and other items. For a project such as this one, he estimated that he would use three weeks of his time and that his commissions would amount to about $2,500. On this basis his consultation fee was set at $300. On some furniture he makes as much as 50 percent commission. On others it is 30 percent, and on a few things only 10 percent. Andrew pays all his expenses, uses the service of an accounting firm, and pays a typist on an hourly basis.

In an average year, Andrew pays income tax on $40,000 net income. He provides all his own insurance and his Individual Retirement Account (IRA) is the only retirement plan he now has in effect. He plans to build his clientele, expanding into the more affluent neighborhoods. He expects to double his present income in five years.

SUGGESTED ADDITIONAL READING

Ball, Victoria Kloss. *Opportunities in Interior Design and Decorating Careers.* Lincolnwood, IL: VGM Career Horizons, 1995.

Dewalt, Suzanne. *How to Open and Operate a Home-Based Interior Design Business.* Old Saybrook, CT: Globe Pequot Press, 1997.

Gardner, Elizabeth B. *Arts and Crafts Careers.* Lincolnwood, IL: VGM Career Horizons, 1998.

CHAPTER 3

HOME ECONOMISTS IN BUSINESS

The very wide range of employment opportunities for home economists includes the exciting and competitive field of business. One of the main differences between home economists in business and those working in other areas is that the business-oriented professional is employed by a profit-making operation. While some home economists are also found in the for-profit sector, countless others operate in the nonprofit or educational sector. Those who are engaged in the business-oriented economy include home economists working in merchandising, hotel/motel and restaurant management, communications companies, and interior design. In fact, many hospitals, family service clinics, and schools also are classified as commercial corporations.

A ROLE IN THE HEART OF A COMPANY

The business home economist is generally employed by manufacturers of food, equipment, or household supplies; energy suppliers; and trade associations. Many work independently as freelance consultants. Even though there may be a common element in their responsibilities, home economics positions can be assigned to any number of corporate departments. Thus, one might find home economists working within a company's research division, developing and testing new products, or in the sales, marketing, or public relations departments, communicating to the public the uses and benefits of a product. Many experienced home economists become a part of the upper management structure of their companies.

WHAT DO HOME ECONOMISTS DO?

Home economists in business are engaged in a very competitive enterprise. They strive to make the product or services of the corporation for which they work a better buy for the consumer than those of rival corporations.

As consumer experts, they use their creativity to help invent and improve products that are attractive, useful, and will sell well. Home economists act as a liaison between the corporate management and consumers. The home economist tries to see things through the eyes of the consumer, and will represent that viewpoint at design and marketing meetings. In this way, they play an instrumental role in product development.

Sometimes companies start their home economists in direct sales. This often entails presenting demonstrations that promote particular products and will involve answering consumer questions. Sales experience is always beneficial in sharpening one's appreciation for the company's contribution to the economy. Home economists are frequently involved in product research and recipe development for both the individual consumer and for institutional use. Other responsibilities include testing equipment as it would be used in the home and training the company's sales force, retail salespeople, and advertisers.

Some companies do basic research, but more often home economists are engaged in applied research that will sharpen the competitive edge of their company. They often work under tight deadlines, as corporations evaluate the worthiness of laboratory projects in a shorter time frame than do government agencies and universities.

The position of home economists in business usually entails a great deal of writing, preparing news releases, preparing labels, and developing use and care books or sales training manuals. Producing printed matter includes preparing food or other subject matter for photography and arranging photographs. Producing attractive pictures of appetizing food—often referred to as food styling—frequently results only after repeated attempts at frying perfect eggs, pouring perfectly round pancakes, successfully unmounding gelatin salads, and the like.

Home economists contribute to the public relations of their company by building good will. They might assist groups, such as Girl Scouts and senior citizens organizations, or help promote events such as athletic marathons and health fairs, by making speeches, setting up exhibits, and preparing other programs.

Major food companies, such as the Quaker Oats Company, Kraft, or General Mills, operate several test kitchens. Teams of home economists develop new products and new uses for well-established products, thus advancing the public's awareness of the product and, thereby, increasing the company's total sales.

Equipment home economists not only help to develop products but also help increase customer acceptance of the products. Home economists have been very involved in the development and distribution of products such as food processors, convection ovens, microwave ovens, automatic washing machines, and freezers. Trade associations frequently employ home economists to promote their products. Thus, the Cotton Council, The Pork Producers Association, National Live Stock and Meat Board, The American Egg Board, and the National Dairy Council have all called upon the professional home economist in their marketing and public outreach efforts.

Home economists working in business frequently travel to other parts of the country and even internationally. Indeed, some positions require being away from home base as much as 50 percent of the time. When home economists travel on behalf of their company, their expenses are paid by the company.

Skills Required

Strong written and oral communication skills are very important in this field. Home economists in business need to have the ability to write clearly and concisely. They relate sales functions to other departments such as research, production, marketing, and advertising. Business home economists need to know how to set up eye-pleasing displays, to communicate the selling points of a product and service, as well as to convey research findings.

Those in business careers must have a high degree of self-discipline and self-confidence. This sort of work calls for an ability to manage time well and the self-discipline to work independently and endure long hours.

PROFESSIONAL ORGANIZATIONS

Among professional organizations, Home Economists in Business (HEIB) holds top priority for professionals in this area. Although it is a part of American Association of Family and Consumer Sciences, it maintains a separate national headquarters. It has separate state and local affiliates and publications. This group was especially active in promoting the certification of home economists. The group maintains active assistance in job placement, both locally and nationally.

Some home economists in business are also members of organizations identified with their specialty, such as advertising, interior design, fashion, hospitality, and tourism. It is important to participate in organizations that maintain a network of communication about such matters as legislation that affects the profession, new government regulations, mass media opportunities, and job openings.

The kinds of corporations that employ home economists will have an increasing importance in an information and service-based economy as opposed to a economy based on heavy industry and manufacturing. The emphasis on human capital indicates an increased demand for the services of home economists.

SALARY

Salary ranges in the commercial sector are quite wide and depend on a person's level of training, years of work for a particular company, and even what industry they work in. Beginners with an undergraduate degree usually start in the low twenty-thousand range. A third of the home economists surveyed reported salaries higher than $30,000 annually, and a fourth in the $25,000 to $30,000 range. A few top executives earn in excess of $100,000.

PROFILE: CONSUMER AFFAIRS PROFESSIONAL

Dave is employed by the consumer affairs division of a major equipment manufacturer. The five-member staff in this department all have a bachelor or master of science degree with majors in textiles, food, or equipment. Dave's desk is in the home economics department, and he shares a laboratory with three other home economists. Over the years, Dave has been involved in a large number of projects. For example, for one project, Dave researched how to best cook fresh broccoli in the microwave. He compared different kinds of utensils, such as glass dishes versus paper ones; he also compared products cooked in tightly covered containers with those wrapped in plastic. A third comparison was made using a rotating platform versus placing the utensil in a stationary position. Another assignment was developing booklets describing the use and care of a microwave oven, which were published by the company for consumer distribution.

Dave also conducts sales training meetings for salespeople in the Northwest. In a typical training week, he will leave the office on Monday afternoon and fly to Portland, where he will conduct the sales meeting on Wednesday. On Tuesday he will set up for the sales training and visit grocery stores to purchase supplies. On Friday he might have another sales training meeting scheduled for San Diego, where he will repeat all the things he did in Portland.

Dave will fly back to his home base Saturday at noon and is expected to be in the office on Monday morning, where his consumer correspondence and e-mails await him.

Dave is also called upon to help deal with consumer problems. For example, he was the consumer liaison for his company when there were numerous complaints concerning cheese being overcooked before the center of the product was hot. Dave experimented with ways to cook the pizza—covered with paper, with plastic, glass, and so on. He answered each letter personally and enclosed one of his leaflets on general company recommendations. He also wrote to manufacturers of frozen pizza alerting them to the problems and giving suggested answers.

After two years with his company Dave was making $28,000 a year with full health insurance, life insurance, and a plan for purchasing company stock at a reduced price. All of his travel expenses are paid by the company, and he has two weeks of paid vacation.

PROFILE: TEST KITCHEN PROFESSIONAL

Kathy works in a test kitchen of a food manufacturer in the Midwest. She came to her job after graduating in foods and nutrition at a land grant college. During her first year her assignments dealt mainly with developing recipes that promote the use of cheese.

First she was asked to experiment with recipes for a cheese souffle that could be packaged, frozen, and then heated in a microwave successfully. Another project was developing a cheese sauce that would hold its flavor and attractiveness for several hours on a buffet table. This sauce was product marketed to institutions such as motels, hotels, restaurants, and caterers. Kathy worked for two months assembling crackers, corn chips, vegetables, and pasta products for which the sauce was an appropriate accompaniment; obtaining attractive photographs, including accessories; and writing promotional material that was then used by the company salespeople.

Another assignment for Kathy was to prepare the package directions for this same cheese sauce. She had to be sure she was using the same standard type of measuring equipment as that used by the hotels or caterers as well as the same thermostatic control on serving equipment.

Kathy's schedule is from 8:30 A.M. until 5:00 P.M. She reports to a test kitchen supervisor who coordinates all food research for the food manufacturer. Her salary is $20,000 a year with company benefits.

SUGGESTED ADDITIONAL READING

Hitch, Elizabeth J. and June Pierce Youatt. *Communicating Family and Consumer Sciences: A Guidebook for Professionals.* Tinley Park, IL: Goodheart-Willcox Co., 1995.

CHAPTER 4

CHILD DEVELOPMENT
AND FAMILY RELATIONS

According to the old African proverb popularized by First Lady Hillary Rodham Clinton, "It takes a village to raise a child." The idea that the welfare of an individual child is the concern of the larger community has long had a place in the American concept of family and society. Home economics is one of the disciplines most concerned with child development and social relations.

EARLY CHILDHOOD EDUCATION

Home economics careers with young children include working directly with children and their parents and training those who care for children in group settings or at home. Preschool education is a term that includes day care, nursery school, and kindergarten.

Preschools are a very large part of the profession of home economics. Until fairly recently, group care and public support for preschool education was scarce in the United States compared with other industrialized countries. Publicly supported kindergartens for five-year-olds became prevalent in urban areas after World War II. Headstart programs for three-year-olds and four-year-olds were organized for disadvantaged children during the 1960s. These programs continue to exist in many communities with some federal support.

A large variety of types of nursery schools is developing. A few with taxpayers' support are located in public schools or community centers. More often the support comes from community organizations such as United Way and must be supplemented by fees paid by the parents.

More than 15 percent of child care centers are run by religious institutions. Others are run by nonprofit organizations or by profit-making companies. An increasing number of businesses offer on-site child care centers for their employees. This is seen as a welcome incentive for working mothers, and it also cuts down on absenteeism. Moreover, it is a valuable way for employers to recruit and retain valued employees.

Some nursery schools are established to provide specific learning opportunities for the children. They are usually characterized by a more highly trained staff and more limited hours of operation.

Most states through their departments of welfare regulate child care services in areas such as sanitation, fire, safety, nutrition, space availability, and minimum training qualifications of staff. There is usually no regulation in employing nannies and babysitters or for caring for a few children in the caretaker's own home.

Directors of day care centers are responsible for the children in their care from early morning until late afternoon. Some centers open as early as 6:00 A.M. so that parents can drop off the child and still get to work on time. Some centers provide bus transportation early in the morning. In these centers breakfast is one of the first activities. Other children arrive at the center after having breakfast at home. The activity schedule will include free time for the children to play with the toys and use the equipment such as swings, slides, and so on. There also will be some directed activity such as story time and time for visitors. There needs to be a teacher for each six or eight children to provide supervision and communication. The younger the child is, the more time he or she requires for physical care. Lunch and snacks, rest, and naps are important aspects of the program. Outdoor activities are a part of the program. There, too, supervision is important. Some of the staff will need to stay late in order that parents may pick up children after work.

Much of what constitutes a person's sense of values is learned as a young child in the informal everyday way things are done or the way conversation takes place. Discipline is an essential ingredient in the training of the child both at home and at school.

For elementary children there is a trend for after-school supervised activities, which may consist of giving a snack or supervising homework and outdoor recreation. These programs are sometimes provided by school corporations, the YMCA, and community centers, and are usually financed by fees paid by parents. Innovative programs for latchkey children provide additional opportunities for home economists to share their knowledge and be involved with young children.

Many child care programs include classes for the parents on how to best care for children in the home. The same teacher who works with the parent may also be the one who works with the children. There is a trend toward emphasis on quality relationship between parent and child. This begins early, even during the pregnancy. Hospitals are offering courses for expectant parents to enhance the opportunity of forging family relationships at the moment of birth. In addition, legislative developments now have established mandatory parental leaves. These will provide time for establishing relationships with children in the important early months following birth.

Trained child development graduates are well equipped to take the initiative in forming preschool organizations. These may be for-profit corporations, not-for-profit companies, or groups within a church or a community center. A home economics background provides an understanding and appreciation for the physical, social, and emotional needs of young children that is not always present in all educational circles. Child development professionals take responsibility for the physical and nutritional facilities, the hiring of staff, and the general operation of the school. Some families with both parents working will give high priority to quality child care and will be willing to compensate those who provide it.

Hospitals are developing child care programs for the benefit of their patients and staff. Many are in operation twenty-four hours a day.

There are also business opportunities for home economists working for corporations that produce children's clothes, furniture, toys, and programs for television. The home economist's challenge is to sell the company on the profitability of satisfying a need with innovative products and services.

For those who aspire to own their own nursery school or child care center, some business skills are essential, such as bookkeeping and the keeping of tax records. In a large operation the manager needs skill in hiring staff, buying equipment and supplies, and managing public relations.

There are some positions that mainly consist of teaching adults about children, such as positions in cooperative extension and those providing parenting classes in community education programs.

Salaries for child care workers depend on the employer and the level of education of the employee. In general, pay is relatively low, though this increases with more education and experience. In 1996 there were more than 1.2 million people employed as preschool teachers and child care workers. Of these, 40 percent were self-employed, primarily as family day care providers. The median earnings for full-time child care workers in 1996 was $250 a week.

FAMILY RELATIONS

Home economists are often referred to as family and consumer science professionals. Those who specialize in family relations will find increased opportunities and challenges. Divorce, single parenting, teenage pregnancy, AIDS, drugs, and alcohol problems in American society create new and varied issues for the family relations professional. Helping individuals understand and adjust to their situation is an important role for home economists. This is usually accomplished through education and counseling.

EDUCATION

Many of those who work with families are employed by community and mental health centers, as well as in family clinics and government agencies. Some of these clinics and programs are independent corporations, some are associated with large hospitals and others are nonprofit organizations funded by government and private grants. Home economics educators in schools and cooperative extension incorporate family living concepts in most courses. Some teachers specialize in the family living curriculum. Adult education departments in high schools, community colleges, the YMCA, and health agencies offer courses in various family living subjects.

Those who are adept in writing for the public will find a ready audience for articles and books in the area of family living. The subject matter areas include, among other things, parenting skills, understanding young children, marital relationships, dealing with teenagers, coping with aged parents, and the drug environment as well as sex education.

COUNSELING

Working one on one with individuals to help them with their personal, family, and social problems is a gratifying aspect of the home economics profession. One important focus of this work is to help people learn how to clearly identify their family values and goals. Values give meaning to life, allowing us to determine the relation between "how it is" and "how we would like it to be."

Professionals who work with families aid their clients in determining the best and most fair distribution of family resources. The professional home economist working in this area will have additional background in the social sciences.

Professional counselors are often engaged in working with couples, helping them to create healthy relationships. They also work with parents and their children. Most family relations involve the entire family rather than just one individual: Good mental health is influenced greatly by positive family relationships.

Counselors usually work on an appointment basis and are often part of a team of specialists. Sometimes it is necessary to have late afternoon and early evening appointments.

Some states regulate the practice of family counseling. The only nationwide standards are those imposed by the

American Association for Marriage and Family Therapy. Their membership includes three categories: clinical, associate, and student. This association has standards for each category of membership and requires supervision of clinical practice by approved supervisors. Additional information can be obtained from the American Association of Marriage and Family Therapy, 1133 Fifteenth Street NW, Suite 300, Washington, DC 20005.

Home economists have long been involved in dealing with the stresses that affect families. All home economists have had courses in health and nutrition, management of family resources, child development, and family relations. Most people can cope with their "away from home" stress if they can return regularly to a comfortable, secure atmosphere at home that is reasonably free of conflict.

The pressures of present-day society have precipitated much concern about managing stress. All home economists, but especially family counselors, can contribute to managing stressful situations.

Counselors with advanced degrees and working full-time can expect beginning salaries from $20,000 to $30,000 annually. This will increase with experience and education to up to about $50,000.

PROFESSIONAL ORGANIZATIONS

For more information on careers working with young children, contact The National Association for the Education of Young Children, 1509 Sixteenth Street NW, Washington, DC 20036; and The Association for Childhood Education International, 11501 Georgia Avenue, Suite 315, Wheaton, MD 20902-1924.

You can learn about eligibility requirements for child care workers by contacting the Council for Early Childhood Professional Recognition, 2460 Sixteenth Street NW, Washington, DC 20009.

PROFILE: CHILD DEVELOPMENT SUPERVISOR

Paulette is assistant to the vice president for personnel of a national insurance company. She works in the company's headquarters in a Midwest city.

Her chief responsibility is the in-house child care program at the headquarters and at four other sites where the company has regional offices. More than 80 percent of all employees in the company's offices are women, so child care is an important aspect of their personnel policy.

The five child-care directors report to Paulette. Each of them has a bachelor's degree in child development; they employ and supervise the staff that works directly with the children. The regional offices have facilities for forty children each; at the home office ninety can be accommodated.

Paulette came to the company ten years ago after working as a teacher in a for-profit franchise. At the school she became acquainted with children's parents, who worked at the insurance headquarters. After some informal conferences she was offered the opportunity to develop an experimental program in a section of a building that was not being used at the time.

The first facilities accommodated only thirty children age two or older. Paulette herself was the head teacher, employing one other degreed teacher, one assistant with an associate degree, and two aides. One aide's responsibility was to see that food for snacks and lunch—ordered by Paulette at the kitchen for the employees' cafeteria—were delivered and served as scheduled. Parents were charged a fee that covered the cost of the staff and supplies. The company absorbed the cost of space and equipment.

Although some employees could find less expensive babysitting at home or with relatives, the high quality of the child care and the convenience to the work site created a strong demand for the program.

When the building was remodeled eight years ago, a nursery for twenty babies ages four to fifteen months was included, and accommodations were provided for up to seventy other children. When each of the regional offices was established, child care was an integral part of the facility.

From the beginning, at least half of Paulette's time was used working with administration on just how the child care was to fit into the compensation of those employees who used it and how the service would actually make the company more profitable.

A liberal parental-leave policy makes it possible for parents to be absent at the time children are born or adopted for as much as six months and still come back to their position. Sick leave may be used for either the employee or his or her child. Nursing mothers arrange their break times to fit the baby's schedule. Parents may arrange to have lunch with their children in the nursery or take the children as their guests to the employees' cafeteria.

Paulette's salary of $50,000 is part of the administration budget. Her total staff budget is $600,000 and comes from fees paid by the parents. The five head teachers average $22,000 per year. The seven associates who hold two-year degrees average $19,000 and the fifteen assistants average $12,000. There are eight part-time helpers who come as needed and are paid $8.00 an hour. The fees also cover food and supplies. The cost of space, utilities, and equipment is still absorbed in the company's budget. The child care staff appreciate their benefit package (which is the same as for all other employees), the reasonable hours, and the encouragement to continue their own professionalism.

Although Paulette has completed a master's degree in business, she identifies herself as a child development home economist and is currently chairperson of the state association.

The insurance company's board of directors is sure that Paulette's program has more than paid for itself. Qualified employees are attracted to the company because of its pro-family policies. In fact, now about one-fourth of the children are brought by their fathers. Employee productivity is above average and absenteeism has been cut to the lowest in the industry.

Although the company's business has more than doubled in the ten years since Paulette has been with them, the number of women employees has only increased 10 percent, mainly because of computerization. However, the now more highly trained employees are more appreciative of quality child care on the premises.

SUGGESTED ADDITIONAL READING

Eberts, Majorie and Margaret Gisler. *Careers for Kids at Heart and Others Who Adore Children.* Lincolnwood, IL: VGM Career Horizons, 1994.
Gallagher, Particia C. *So You Want to Open a Profitable Child Care Center.* St. Louis, MO: Mosley-Year Book, 1994.
Wittenberg, Renee. *Opportunities in Child Care Careers.* Lincolnwood, IL: VGM Career Horizons, 1994.

CHAPTER 5

COMMUNICATIONS, JOURNALISM, AND ADVERTISING

Few professions are as exciting and challenging as working in the realm of communications. Here you will be in touch with the most up-to-date information on developments in the field of home economics. If you work as a journalist, your job will be to convey the news and developments to an eager and interested public. The topics that relate to families and consumers appeal to a large segment of the American public, and reporters in these fields can work for a wide range of publications.

In a communications job such as public relations, the task can be as varied as lobbying United States Congress regarding pending legislature, to helping organize public service campaigns. National trade organizations such as the Dairy Council or the American Pork Producers employ communications experts to help spread their messages and to create newsletters and brochures that are exchanged within the industry.

Jobs in advertising similarly require strong writing skills and creativity, whether you are working in-house at a large company or at an ad agency hired to promote a particular project. By combining a strong training in marketing with a specialization in family and consumer sciences, one would be well positioned to create memorable, effective ad campaigns.

JOBS IN COMMUNICATIONS AND JOURNALISM

Many newspapers and magazines have a special department dedicated to issues that concern families and consumers, such as food, health, fashions, home furnishings, consumer affairs, and others. At smaller organizations, the same person edits or writes all the articles in these areas.

If you work in a specialized area or cover more general topics, it is important that you have a strong and broad education. Home economics will provide you with the special knowledge regarding these topics and also will give you the tools for creative thinking. You will do well to study history, English, philosophy, or any other liberal arts or science topics.

As you would expect, jobs in communications call for a strong talent as a writer. Great satisfaction results from knowing one's audience and being able to articulate information in a way that readers will understand and be able to use in their daily lives. Unlike teachers, media educators usually have only one chance to get their message through, and so must be clear and concise.

A number of home economists write columns for local newspapers, and some of these columns are syndicated for publications throughout the country. These may be written in the home and constitute only a part-time job. The wider the circulation, the more correspondence is required.

A home economist's background makes it possible to integrate the functions of the product or services being promoted into the total consumer picture. This may be using products in the home and working with a select group of people who evaluate what's new. As lifestyles change, there is a need for constant updating of familiar products and services. A home economics communicator needs to know the audience and the way they live.

The daily tasks require the necessity of meeting deadlines and using good judgment in selecting the most appropriate information from the vast amount of both educational and promotional material submitted. Keeping one's professional integrity requires constant attention. National travel and conventions are on the agenda of most experienced home economists in communication at least once or twice a year.

Skill in interviewing is important to those who write as well as those who work in radio and TV. Knowing what questions to ask in order to get the information that is needed or appropriate to the situation comes with experience.

Home economists working in the electronic media may be employees of the broadcasting station or of advertising agencies or of manufactures. This is an area in which freelance home economists may find their clients. Keeping abreast of all that is new in products and services for the home and with the changing needs and interests of homemakers is basic to success in these positions. The work demands enthusiasm, vision, and a capacity for sustained interest.

A home economist who has her or his own show must have strong executive and managerial skills. It is essential to keep accurate records of products and equipment used as well as sponsors of the programs and guests. Topics and guests are scheduled several weeks or months in advance. Appealing programs attract additional sponsors. A big part of the job on a program is answering mail and telephone calls. Responsibilities also include making public appearances, being gracious, being able to respond quickly, having a pleasant speaking voice, and being well groomed.

Using photography to communicate consumer messages is a part of many home economics jobs. This includes television, use and care booklets, displays, slide film strips, and magazine and newspaper photos. Some home economists operate the camera themselves, but the majority work with a professional photographer either performing or preparing material to be photographed. Designing the setting for the television presentation, accumulating props for demonstration, arranging for models, and preparing food that will be photographed are all part of the job.

ADVERTISING

A home economist working in advertising may be employed by an advertising agency, by a producer, or by a trade association. A freelance home economist may contract with businesses to prepare their advertising. Advertising media include newspapers, magazines, television, radio, direct mail, exhibits, billboards, and educational material.

A home economist working in an advertising agency may be assigned three or four accounts at the same time. For example, he or she might be working with a manufacturer of lamps, detergents, cookies, and toys. This makes for variety and is challenging. It also provides opportunities for obtaining new accounts. These people work with copywriters, marketing specialists, account executives, and other professionals. If a client has an advertising department, the home economist will work directly with that department. The home economist works with newspaper editors in order to have a news article that describes the client's product. He or she may also help to get the client on talk shows.

An advertising agency with food accounts may have its own test kitchen. A part of the home economist's job may be to create new uses of the products being promoted. Sometimes taste panels will be conducted to promote new products. A firm may rely on its advertising agency to develop packaging designs and label information.

Public relations skills such as being a pleasant conversationalist, enjoying making new contacts, and having a good appearance are a plus for this job. These skills may serve as stepping stones to becoming an account executive.

Some of the home economics positions in communications are involved in research. Recipe writing evolves from test kitchen research; the latest appliances and their use should be tried out in practical applications; experience is necessary with the latest in laundry and cleaning supplies and services. Newspapers, national magazines, radio, and television protect their reputation by using reliable sources of information or doing on-site testing.

Salaries follow the pattern of the employer. Not-for-profit organizations follow a salary schedule based on education and experience. In profit making organizations a home economist may climb to a top executive position.

PROFESSIONAL ORGANIZATIONS

To learn more about internships, scholarships, and journalism careers, contact The Dow Jones Newspaper Fund, P. O. Box 300, Princeton, NJ 08540.

The Public Relations Society of America publishes a comprehensive directory of schools offering studies in public relations and advertising. You can receive the brochure, "Where Shall I Go to Study Advertising and Public Relations" for $5.00 by writing to: The Public Relations Society of America, Inc., 33 Irving Place, New York, NY 10003-2376.

JOB OUTLOOK

The beginning salary for a writer at a newspaper or magazine is approximately $21,000 a year. Those who have been employed for more than five years average about $30,000 a year, although senior writers and editors earn over $67,000 a year. Because so many people are interested in working in this exciting field, the competition is quite strong. However, the growth of the Internet and other nontraditional media sources will allow for talented, creative writers to find a niche in this burgeoning industry. Many writers will continue to work on a freelance basis, often contracting with a number of publications or organizations.

Public relations specialists earn an average salary of about $34,000 a year, although the top 10 percent earned more than $75,000 a year in 1996. This is a very competitive field, attracting a large number of applicants with college backgrounds. Employment in public relations is expected to increase faster than average through the year 2000, as people retire or leave the occupation to take another job. A person with an education combining public relations and home economics would be well-suited to pursue careers at companies that focus on consumer and family-oriented businesses and organizations.

PROFILE: FOODS COLUMNIST

Mary is a good example of how a home economist's career can be very flexible and interesting. Regardless of age, family situation, location, or minor physical handicaps, it is usually possible to find or create a position.

Mary is middle-aged and well into her second home economics career. Because of an accident that resulted in limiting her driving to daytime, she took an early retirement from her 4-H position.

She had become a 4-H agent right out of college. She enjoyed studying foods, and for the last ten years she worked with extension, she was the regional foods agent for her county. The retirement program into which she had deposited a percentage of her income along with the contribution of her university made an early retirement possible. Although her monthly check—tied to the Consumer Price Index—is quite modest, under $2,000 a month after federal income tax is taken out, it is enough for her to maintain the basics of her lifestyle.

Her new career as a foods columnist fits her situation perfectly. She was well known throughout the metropolitan area of the city where she lives as a result of her extension work. The major newspaper there has a food section on Sundays and Wednesdays and agreed to print a column with recipes. She tests every recipe (as well as many that do not get in the paper) in her own kitchen. Her apartment is near a group home for mildly handicapped young people, so she never lacks for someone to taste her experiments and provide comments on her products.

Eventually the phone calls to the paper about her column exceeded the number a secretary for the newspaper could comfortably handle. Mary was then asked to appear once a week for the morning call-in radio show. The radio station and the newspaper belong to the same corporation. The radio program has now grown to an hour, five mornings a week. Callers are encouraged to stick to topics in her printed columns, but she sometimes introduces new ideas, suggestions, and advice on other foods and nutrition subjects that are pertinent to the season or the consumer situation. She spends an hour or more each morning in the office of the radio station taking care of correspondence. She is amazed at the number of food companies that want her to promote their products and specify them in her recipes.

Her style is "folksie" but her reputation for reliability was quickly established. When she doesn't know the answer she says so; then she hunts for it and reports it in a later program.

The money she earns as a columnist, on average a little more than $2,000 a month, she is able to save in a tax-free retirement fund. The actual amount earned varies because she is paid by the column-inch for her newspaper work. The corporation sent her to two conventions for food editors last year, allowing her to travel to Chicago and Dallas and meet and speak with colleagues in her field.

SUGGESTED ADDITIONAL READING

Agrawal, Hema. *Society, Culture, and Mass Communication: Sociology of Journalism.* Columbia, MO: Har-Anard Pubns., 1995.
Charity, Arthur. *Doing Public Journalism.* New York: Guilford Pubns., 1995.

CHAPTER 6

HUMAN SERVICES

One of the hallmarks of a career in home economics is that it involves working in human services. As we have seen in earlier chapters, this can take the form of very close contact with the client, as in child care, interior decorating, or education, or more indirect service, such as public relations or journalism.

In this chapter we will examine careers that provide home economists with the opportunity to work intimately with specific groups, such as the elderly, poor, or handicapped, or with populations in the Third World. Most of the job opportunities with disadvantaged, elderly, or handicapped clients, as well as those overseas, are to be found with nonprofit or government agencies, although positions also exist at for-profit hospitals, schools, and other types of service agencies.

Experts in family and consumer sciences, nutritionists, and other home economics specialists often are employed by public health and welfare departments. Here the home economist may provide education and counseling to the recipients of benefits, encouraging them in their efforts to become more fully independent. Other home economists work for public housing authorities, nursing homes, community centers, churches, as well as residential and nonresidential centers that serve elderly or handicapped clients.

These jobs are almost uniformly demanding, and usually one cannot expect much in the way of monetary compensation. The rewards for those who work in these fields are more of a profound, personal nature—the satisfaction of contributing one's energies and expertise to help improve the lives of others.

REHABILITATION

Those working in rehabilitation may work with individual physically handicapped clients to develop ways they can prepare their own food, dress themselves, arrange functional living quarters for their use, and make sure they can take their own medicine.

The home economist in rehabilitation work teaches and motivates the clients to use home living practices that make for independence. In large institutions home economists may develop clothing and kitchen tools that are adapted for the handicapped.

In residential situations home economists may work as consultants or as managers. A part of their responsibility is to see that the physical facilities are maintained. This includes meeting safety and health standards; if the home economist is a manager, he or she may employ and train other staff to assist residents in their daily living needs. The disability of the client may be physical, mental, or emotional. In recent years working with drug- and alcohol-related problems has become a large part of rehabilitation. Solving problems with a client almost always involves working with the client's family. Home economists' appreciation of family relations and nutrition makes them especially suited for positions in this field. Usually the home economist works as part of a team made up of medical doctors, nurses, psychologists, and their assistants. The basic purpose of the rehabilitation program is to help the client become independent.

COMMUNITY CENTERS

Park departments and community centers frequently offer educational opportunities in home economics to both adults and young people. Most of these positions are part-time and offer good hourly pay plus personal satisfaction and experience.

HOMEMAKER SERVICE

Homemaking services are offered through social welfare agencies for families temporarily unable to supply these services for themselves. Their inability may be due to the hospitalization of the mother, death of a spouse, aging, or extensive travel and work schedules of both parents. The service needed may be as infrequent as once a week or as demanding as a full-time live-in situation. The types of work encompassed include food preparation, light housekeeping and laundry, marketing, and child care. With the use of homemaker service it is often possible for a family to remain intact through a very stressful situation.

The professional home economist supervises the work of paraprofessionals who go into the home to do the work. The training of the paraprofessional is the responsibility of the home economist. Usually the home economist makes an initial visit to determine what services are needed and to estimate the amount of time that is required. Some follow-up and evaluation visits may be required by the home economist.

In smaller agencies the home economist may work out the schedule for paraprofessionals, who are often called homemakers. People employed as homemakers receive fringe benefits such as social security, group health insurance, paid vacations, and at least minimum wage. They are respected by the community because of the high standards that are maintained.

Sometimes homemaker service is combined with visiting nurse services and with meals on wheels. For example, a widower may be able to maintain life in his own home with a five-day-a-week delivery of meals on wheels, a one-day-a-week drop-in by a visiting nurse, and a half day a week of homemaker service for housekeeping, laundry, and so on.

Another example might be a five-day job from three to five in the afternoon where schoolchildren have after-school supervision and the evening meal is ready to be served when the parents get home.

THE PEACE CORPS

In the last three decades the Peace Corps, which describes itself as "The Toughest Job You'll Ever Love," has offered exciting opportunities in home economics all over the world. The positions are challenging and require maturity and responsibility. Both the young and the experienced have responded and continue to respond to the challenge of helping to improve home life in developing countries. Because of language cultural differences, a special training period is given by the government. A person who succeeds in these positions should be innovative, flexible, and have good health.

Churches also offer positions for home economists in their overseas missions programs.

Additional Information

State and local social service agencies can provide you with information on opportunities in homemaker services. You can receive information on certification and training from The National Association for Home Care, 228 Seventh Street SE, Washington, DC 20003.

Information on careers as a home health aide, and data on schools offering training, are available from The National Association of Health Career Schools, 750 First Street NE, Suite 940, Washington, DC 20002.

To learn more about the Peace Corps, you can visit the organization's web site, where you will find in-depth stories from volunteers as well as program descriptions. The home page address is: www.peacecorps.gov. For the contact information for your state, call 1-800-424-8580 or write Peace Corps, 1111 Twentieth Street NW, Washington, DC 20526.

AGING

Since the establishment of the Administration on Aging by the federal government, professional opportunities for people with knowledge and skills in gerontology have been greatly expanded. Regional, state, and some county offices on aging are spread throughout the country. Many of the programs provided by local community centers such as day care services, senior nutrition programs, retired senior volunteer programs, and older worker employment programs are usually at least partially funded through the federal agencies. Home economists are employed both as managers and as specialists in these programs.

Home economists working with the elderly may be employed by retirement homes or nursing centers, the YMCA, park and recreation departments, insurance companies, and travel agencies.

Home economists may be part of a team employed by community colleges, the YMCA, financial institutions, or by large corporations to operate preretirement planning programs and to do retirement counseling. An important contribution of the home economist to these programs is to help clients make rational decisions on whether to maintain their own household, share a home with another family member, move into an apartment, or become part of a retirement community complex. Home economists will also help seniors evaluate what kind of services are desirable to their particular needs.

Home economists are also very involved in guiding people toward proper, healthy nutrition. In the nursing home or residential setting, this involves planning menus that are appropriate, digestible, and well balanced nutritionally. Home economists are often occupied in jobs that provide recreation and craft exercises to elderly clients.

Another service in which the home economist can assist is that of personal shopper. Sometimes this may involve taking people on shopping trips; sometimes it involves actually doing the shopping for them. It may involve supplying them with catalogs and helping them make out their orders. This may be for personal supplies or gifts for their grandchildren. Acting as a shopping consultant—helping stretch scarce dollars—can be especially helpful, for example by locating generic drugs.

CASE MANAGEMENT

Helping the elderly obtain services to which they are entitled such as Medicaid, Medicare, housing assistance, disability compensation, food stamps, legal and energy assistance, and helping them avail themselves of suitable private programs is an appropriate task for the home economist.

As the percentage of retired persons increases, due to demographic surges as well as better health care, there is a growing demand for home care services. That demand is expected to increase as elderly people become a larger proportion of the population and as state governments develop systems that make such services available and affordable. Many states have home care services as a part of either aging, health, or welfare departments.

In 1996, homemaker-home health aides held about 697,000 jobs. This number is rising rapidly, and home care services will be one of the fastest-growing occupations through the year 2006.

The designation *case management* is being used to describe the function of assessing need and coordinating services to fulfill the need. Payment for the services is usually on a sliding scale. Funds come from programs such as

Medicare, Medicaid, state and federal grants, private insurance, health associations, and individual private payment. The home economist working in case management cooperates with health professionals.

Home economists are especially sensitive to the need for close personal relationships. They are well equipped to assist in programs such as foster grandparents, which offer a substitute affection for family members.

PROFESSIONAL ORGANIZATIONS

Professional organizations include:

National Association of Social Workers
750 First Street NE, Suite 700
Washington, DC 20002-4241
Internet address: www.naswdc.org

The American Association of Retired Persons
601 E Street NW
Washington, DC 20049
Internet address: www.aarp.org

SALARY

The salary may begin very low; Peace Corps people are considered to be volunteers in their very modest compensation. Beginning salaries in rehabilitation and aging organizations may be as low as $12,000 annually or $6.95 an hour.

However, those with more responsibility in larger organizations earn two or three times as much.

PROFILE: ACTIVITIES DIRECTOR

Carol is very pleased with her situation. She is the activities director in two retirement homes in her suburban town of twenty-two thousand people. The Lutheran home is organized as a not-for-profit corporation of her own church—the other is a unit of a national for-profit franchise. Each has approximately 150 residents at any given date. Her contracts call for approximately sixty hours work per month at each institution. One stipulates not less than ten hours per week. She sometimes makes phone calls and does planning at home.

Her responsibilities include arranging and promoting social and recreational activities for the residents. She cooperates with the dietitian and kitchen staff in planning special meals and in planning parties. She also arranges for some residents to occasionally prepare their specialty in the kitchen and then share with other residents. Handicraft classes include the ones she teaches herself and others that are led by volunteers whom she coordinates.

At least once every month there are events for guests such as a Mother's Day tea, holiday bazaars, summer fairs, and patriotic celebrations. Part of her responsibility is to visit with residents, evaluate their need for help in the area of family and social relations, and consult with the other professional staff.

One real benefit of the job is the way it fits into her own family life. Carol had resigned from teaching clothing in a junior high in the spring before her son—who is now eight—was born. She had planned to give full-time to homemaking. Her son was only two and a half when she was asked about accepting the part-time position at the Lutheran home. She was encouraged to bring him with her to the home whenever she felt it would be good for him or the residents. A crib was provided so he could nap there, and often his presence made the "party of the day" a success. Carol's second child, a daughter, is now three. She, too, has become part of the Lutheran home family. Her son's Cub Scout troup meets at the other home where they have six sponsoring "grandpas." The flexibility of the hours is more of an advantage than a disadvantage. However, there are times when she must employ a babysitter, and she may be involved as much as two evenings a month on the job.

Compensation is not large for either position, but her combined salaries amount to the mid-teens. She is not required to participate in any insurance or retirement program. This is a plus for her because her husband has excellent family coverage with his company.

Carol is now discussing with the management of her second company the possibility of incorporating a child care program into the services it offers. She believes the opportunity for quality child care and elder care can both be enhanced if they share some activities. It would mean some changes in the facilities and would require qualified staff such as herself. She is studying for a master's degree in geriatrics and expects to work full-time after her daughter is in school.

SUGGESTED ADDITIONAL READING

Jones-Lee, Anita and Melanie Callender. *The Complete Book to Eldercare.* New York: Barrons Educational Series, 1998.

Skala, Ken. *American Guidance for Seniors and Their Caregivers.* Chevy Chase, MD: Key Communications Group, 1998.

Wykle, May L. and Amasa B. Ford. *Serving Minority Elders in the Twenty-First Century.* New York: Springer Publishers, 1998.

CHAPTER 7

DIETETICS: FOOD AND NUTRITION FOR BETTER HEALTH

"Eat right" has become a rallying cry for professionals concerned with the dietary habits of Americans. Although the connection between good nutrition and better health has long been observed, this message is harder to get across to a population that is deluged with advertisements for sweetened and high-fat food products. Unfortunately, the result is that over 50 percent of the American population is classified as overweight or even obese. Poor dietary habits lead to increased rates of heart disease and other life-threatening illnesses.

Dietetics is the science of applying food and nutrition to health. Dietitians are the well-trained and respected professionals who help people learn how to have a healthier lifestyle through good nutrition. The term "dietitian" was first defined in 1899, at a conference on home economics. It was determined that the title "dietitian" should be "applied to persons who specialize in the knowledge of food and can meet the demands of the medical profession for diet therapy."

By the turn of the century, courses in nutrition and dietetics were being taught in colleges throughout the United

States. Many of these programs grew out of home economics programs. In the early years, one of the primary forums for exchanging information about the new field was the annual national meetings of the American Home Economics Association, which was started in 1909.

The integral role of home economics in the field of dietetics continues to this day. Now dietitians, who are either *registered dietitians* (RD) or *dietetic technicians, registered* (DTR) work in health care, education, and research. Many are employed by the government, and scores more work in restaurant management, for food producers, and in private companies such as fitness organizations.

The field of dietetics is divided into several specialty areas.

GENERAL PRACTITIONERS

General practitioners of dietetics are often the only dietitian in the institutions where they are employed. These may be small hospitals, medical centers, colleges, or profit-making corporations. A dietitian may be employed by two or more nursing homes or extended care facilities. Some dietitians function as freelance professionals or dietetic consultants. The dietitian could be a consultant for nursing homes, meals on wheels services, children's homes, detention facilities, or corporations producing specialty foods.

In these varied settings the dietitian is part of the health care team; he or she tries to educate patients about nutrition and also administers medical nutrition therapy. The dietitian also may manage the food service operation in order to ensure that it follows good dietary guidelines.

To be successful the generalist must be adaptable, qualified, and self-disciplined. She or he must have administrative, educational, and clinical competencies. The generalist has the opportunity to be creative in marketing his or her skills. The flexibility of such employment is advantageous for those who wish to combine a career with homemaking or with continued study. During a time when mobility is important, this phase of dietetics is good for part-time employment.

MANAGEMENT DIETITIANS

The administrative dietitian may be defined as a member of the management team that affects the nutritional care of groups through the management of food service systems that provide optimal nutrition and quality food.

Institutions employing administrative dietitians are usually large enough to have a complex food management system that may include satellite units. Management dietitians are called upon to oversee large-scale meal planning and preparation for health care facilities such as hospitals, company cafeterias, and schools. Functioning in such positions involves sharing responsibility as part of the management team.

Skills involve solving problems in food availability and staff planning, understanding expectations of clients or patients, and complying with government regulations. Dietitians who function as administrators have usually served in several less responsible positions before being advanced to the administrative level.

Those who aspire to administrative positions will need more training or experience in business administration, social and cultural aspects of food, labor relations, and legal responsibilities. Often the head dietitian will need to be able to convince his or her administrators of the importance of nutrition in the recovery or continued health of the client. This is the kind of position for the person who is a self-starter, likes responsibility, and is willing to put in long hours.

CLINICAL DIETITIANS

The clinical dietitian applies the science and art of human nutrition in helping individuals and groups attain optimal health. They are most often employed in hospitals and nursing homes.

Clinical dietitians who work in the treatment of the ill are sometimes called therapeutic dietitians. The individual who enjoys the scientific aspects of nutrition will probably be happiest in this type of work. The work will involve planning specific diets for special needs. It may involve gathering, evaluating, and reporting client-based data. It also may involve adapting and interpreting physicians' orders. Some clinical dietitians specialize in the nutritional guidance of overweight patients or in the care of diabetic or critically ill patients.

The dietitian may act as a teacher or as a counselor for patients, for their families, or for groups. Most clinical dietitians work in hospitals or medical centers. Persons in this specialization will need to be better educated in biology and chemistry than other dietitians.

COMMUNITY DIETITIANS

Community dietitians provide counseling to individuals and groups and usually work for the state, county, or city health departments. Much of their work is educational in nature, helping people acquire the nutritional information to prevent disease and promote good health. They may be asked to take a leadership role in programs to produce change in food practices. This may include nutritional assessment, referrals, and advocacy. An example might be a nutritionist employed by a city health department whose duties include working with pregnant teenagers, referring them to programs such as W. I. C., in which the federal government provides food coupons and other health services. Another aspect of such positions might be encouraging senior citizens to use inexpensive or available surplus foods. On occasion community dietitians may be asked to testify before state legislative committees, or they may take the initiative in finding ways to provide needed food services such as organizing food banks and pantries.

EXPANDING ROLES OF DIETITIANS

Dietitians have established unique roles in a variety of settings.

Increased public awareness of the importance of nutrition and weight control will encourage health maintenance organizations and physical fitness clubs to employ the services of a nutritionist. Skills needed in this field include communications, public relations, and human motivation as well as empathy with people of diverse backgrounds.

Supportive Personnel

Supportive personnel that work with the dietitian include both the dietary manager and dietetic technician. The latter term was created by the American Dietetic Association for those with academic preparation equivalent to two years of classroom instruction (usually leading to an associate degree) and a minimum of 450 hours of supervised field experience. Dietetic technicians could be trained in food service management, nutritional care, or as a generalist.

Dietary managers are persons recognized by the Hospital, Institution and Educational Food Service Society. Both dietary managers and dietary technicians are recognized by the federal government and in many cases perform similar roles.

Dietetic technicians in food service supervise food production and services. Dietetic technicians in nutrition care assist in providing patient services such as planning menus, taking diet history, calculating routine modified diets, and teaching normal nutritional habits.

CERTIFICATION

To become a dietitian or nutritionist requires a bachelor's degree with a major in dietetics, foods and nutrition, food services systems management, or home economics.

There are two major routes in which universities and colleges prepare students to be dietitians. The traditional pattern includes an internship of from six to eighteen months following the completion of a bachelor's degree. The coordinated undergraduate program includes 900 to 1,100 hours of supervised correlated clinical experience during the completion of the baccalaureate degree.

The basic requirements for the dietetics specialization include chemistry (inorganic and organic), human physiology, microbiology, sociology, psychology, economics, writing (creative or technical), mathematics to intermediate algebra, and learning theory or educational methods. Courses in food and nutrition include food preparation, food composition, food chemistry, diet and disease, nutrition values, and nutrition management, theory, and principles. Each area of specialization will have additional course requirements.

Registration or certification is a function of professional organizations. It is done to ensure the competency of its members and to protect society in general from frauds or quacks.

The training of a dietitian must be carried out at a university or college program approved by the Commission on

Accreditation Approval for Dietetics Education (CAADE) of the American Dietetic Association.

According to the American Dietetic Association (ADA), for dietitians "to achieve registration status, the applicant must hold at least a bachelor's degree from an accredited college or university, must have completed certain specific academic and experiential components, must have the appropriate endorsement to verify the completion of these requirements, must pay an initial fee, and must receive a passing score on the national registration examinations."

Registered dietitians are required to constantly update their training with workshops, seminars, independent study, and academic classes.

The American Dietetic Association serves as the primary channel for public service and the advancement of dietetics. It was founded in 1917 and has been copied in many other countries.

The American Dietetic Association develops competencies expected of students and establishes standards for college and university accreditation. Once dietitians are registered with the association, they are allowed to add the R.D. following their names.

SALARY AND JOB OUTLOOK

Employment of dietitians is expected to grow about as fast as the average for all occupations through the year 2006. This is mainly due to an increased interest and emphasis on preventing disease by improving health habits.

Salary levels for dietitians vary widely with geographic location. In 1997, the annual base salary of full-time dietitians working in hospitals was $34,400. Salaries of dietitians in metropolitan areas go as high as $50,000 with several years of experience and advanced training. The median annual income for registered dietitians in 1995 varied by practice area. Thus, clinical nutritionists averaged $34,131; food and nutritional management $42,964; community nutrition $33,902; consultation and business $43,374; and education and research $42,784.

The ADA controls the use of the trademark R.D. and maintains records of paid membership and the accumulation of continuing education hours.

PROFESSIONAL ORGANIZATIONS

The American Dietetic Association can be contacted at 216 West Jackson Blvd., Suite 800, Chicago, IL 60606-6995. The ADA home page is: www.eatright.org.

PROFILE: HEALTH CLUB DIRECTOR

When Mark unlocks his office door he is proud to see the letters "R.D." after his name. He has been associate director of this health club, owned by a partnership of four medical doctors, since it opened three years ago. The doctors work together at a nearby clinic in an affluent village that is part of a large metropolitan area.

Most of Mark's clients are referred to him by the clinic. They participate in exercise programs and group weight control classes that he teaches and confer with him regularly about their weight or their eating habits. He is at the club forty-five to fifty-five hours a week, but despite the long hours he enjoys his work. He usually has three or four classes of six to eight persons in progress. They meet once a week for forty-five minutes for six weeks. There is usually at least one high-school-age class meeting at 4:00 in the afternoon, a morning class that may have young homemakers or retirees, and an evening class that accommodates career people after work.

Mark's work includes the management of a restaurant that enhances the club. The menu always lists calories as well as price and often provides additional nutrition information. The chef and an assistant work directly under Mark's supervision. Clients appreciate the convenience and the high quality of the food served. The reputation of the restaurant has expanded beyond the club clientele and has become a popular place for both lunch and dinner.

Mark got acquainted with the doctors who own the club when they were all working at a downtown hospital. He had just finished his internship and was anxious to expand the role of nutrition in the health care and maintenance of all the patients. One of the doctors shared his enthusiasm for the importance of food and convinced the other three that Mark would be an asset in their venture into the health care business.

Mark was amazed when he was offered a position in their new business. He was not as delighted with hospital life in a big city as he had expected to be and decided that this chance to live and work in a different setting was worth the risk. He has had no regrets. He enjoys patients who are not critically ill and the variety of consulting, teaching, and management that make up his day and his irregular schedule.

His salary in the low $30,000s is low for the community, but it is about what he would have at this stage if he had stayed at the hospital. He likes the respect these doctors give his profession and the way they appreciate his contribution to the business success of the health club. The salary is more than enough for Mark to maintain a lifestyle he feels is appropriate—he uses the club himself—and he is provided excellent health insurance and does not need to spend much on transportation. His schedule can be adjusted to accommodate the activities of professional associations, cultural and social engagements, and occasional long weekends with his family in another part of the state.

Recently Mark worked out an agreement with the director that will permit him to share in the profits of the club. The doctors had expected to use losses on the club as income tax write-offs for the first four or five years, but the third year showed a small profit.

PROFILE: PRODUCT
DEVELOPMENT COORDINATOR

Virginia's company, a producer of top-quality canned and frozen fruits and vegetables, has decided to enter the market for packaged convenience foods. One of the products is to be a line of 300-calorie meals.

Since Virginia had been responsible for developing several of the company's successful combinations and servings of foods, she was asked to head the team that would develop the new line of products. As an undergraduate in home economics, her emphasis was in nutrition and experimental foods. This training and her work experience especially qualify her for the task.

Virginia has been provided with two assistants and the use of a test kitchen and laboratory. First of all they will determine the meat or protein product to be featured in each meal. The accompanying fruit and vegetable servings will probably be those they are already producing. Controlling the size of the portions and the amount of fat on the meat will be essential in controlling the calories. They will study the competitive products now on the market and make sure that theirs look more attractive, give more variety, or appeal to a different clientele.

Nutrition information on the package will include calories, vitamins, and minerals for each item.

Virginia also will work with the packaging department in developing a suitable and attractive package that can go directly into the microwave or the conventional oven and also be used for serving.

Virginia sees this new assignment as her opportunity to move up the corporate ladder. She visualizes making a product that will not only sell in grocery stores but will also be popular at neighborhood convenience stores, health food stores, and delicatessens.

SUGGESTED ADDITIONAL READING

Caldwell, Carol Coles. *Opportunities in Nutrition Careers.* Lincolnwood, IL: VGM Career Horizons, 1991.
Sims-Bell, Barbara. *Career Opportunities in the Food and Beverage Industry.* New York: Facts on File, 1995.

CHAPTER 8

THE HOSPITALITY INDUSTRY: CREATING POSITIVE EXPERIENCES

Whether you are traveling on business or with your family, you expect to be treated to a certain level of service. You want the hotel you have chosen to have an efficient check-in and check-out procedure for guests, and clean, well-lit, and comfortable rooms. Depending on your needs, you also may require a reliable wake-up service, properly equipped rooms for business meetings, or any number of other personalized services, from dry-cleaning to help with purchasing Broadway theater tickets.

In short, what travelers pay for at the hotels and motels where they lodge is "hospitality." The hospitality industry—which includes institutional, hotel, motel, and restaurant management—is a dynamic, exciting business. It is found in every part of the United States providing lodging and meals at all price ranges, from the highway motel to the most luxurious residential suites, and from the local diner to the four-star restaurant. The hospitality industry calls for long hours, enormous reservoirs of patience, and the ability to deal with nearly any kind of immediate crisis.

This industry is closely connected to the fortunes of the business world. During periods of robust economy, more people will travel and eat out, at business lunches and dinners, and on their own personal time, as they have less time to prepare meals at home and more income to spend at restaurants. In many parts of the country, tourism revenues have come to replace agricultural or industrial economies. As opportunities for employment in manufacturing grow smaller, the possibilities expand for tourist-related events, such as conventions and festivals. In fact, the tourism industry is now the second-largest employer in the United States.

The hospitality industry reflects other trends in American society as well. For example, according to the Travel Industry Association, women now account for 40 percent of all business travelers. Whereas once primarily men traveled for business, within a few years it is expected that women travelers will make up the majority of business guests at hotels and motels. The hospitality industry is responding to these changes with intensified efforts to better understand the real needs of their customers.

WIDE RANGE OF OPPORTUNITIES

Hotel and motel managers are in charge of making their establishments run efficiently and profitably. At a small motel or inn, the manager may be responsible for all aspects of the operation. Large hotels may be staffed by hundreds of workers and supervised by a dozen or more departmental managers.

Positions other than administration include personnel training such as housekeeping, laundry, and equipment maintenance. Other positions are tourist directors, executive housekeepers, facility designers, and consultants.

The administrators have the responsibility to make the business profitable and to maintain a good management-labor relationship. In smaller institutions, the administrator also may be the personnel trainer and the executive house-keeper. Expertise in efficiency with workers and equipment may mean the difference between profit and loss.

FOOD SERVICE

Food service is an integral part of all hospitality. It is sometimes defined as a team that encompasses all types of establishments supplying and preparing food for consumption away from home.

Positions

Large restaurants employ general managers, one or more assistant managers, and usually an executive chef.

Positions in food service can be divided into those dealing with actual production of food, serving the food, and managing the business. Usually the chef is head of the kitchen.

In large operations there may be an executive chef or a production manager who has support chefs. Under the chefs there are cooks, specialized cooks such as bakers, salad makers, pantry supervisors, and even meat cutters. Lesser positions are usually called assistant cooks and clean-up and maintenance employees.

The head of the dining room may be called the dining room manager, the food service supervisor, hostess, or maître d'hôtel (popularly maître d'). Waiters, waitresses, bus personnel, and cashiers usually work under the supervision of the dining room head.

The business may be controlled by a manager or a management team. A large operation must include one or more assistant managers. Sometimes there is a purchasing agent and sometimes an executive chef and a food production manager who is considered part of top management.

The manager needs to know and understand every aspect of the operation. Those who do well in this demanding position must have drive, commitment, and long-range goals. Most managers will employ and either train or designate someone to train and supervise new employees. The manager must know the market in which he or she operates and control all office procedures. This would include quantity and quality of food ordered, cost controls, sanitary regulations, advertising, and promotion. An energetic person who generally likes people and is competent to deal fairly with emergencies will be respected by the other employees and earn a profit for the company.

The production manager or the executive chef is responsible for all food preparation. This person must have leadership skills to deal with supervising all kitchen staff, sanitation standards, and cost control methods. Success also depends on creativity in both meals and recipe development and in serving. Having a flair for the unusual and attractive and service helps to promote the business.

The chef and her or his assistants prepare and portion out all food served. In large operations there may be chefs specializing in meats and sauces, vegetables and soups, salads, desserts, and breads.

The dining room manager supervises all dining room staff and activity including staff training for waiters and waitresses, bus personnel, and cashiers. In smaller operations they will greet customers, take reservations, handle complaints, and ensure order and cleanliness in the dining room.

Success in this position requires skill in organization, politeness, and ease in dealing with the public. The best dining room managers are distinguished by a knowledge of etiquette, a neat appearance, and the ability to surround themselves with competent help and satisfied guests. Waiters and waitresses take orders, frequently make suggestions to customers, serve the food, and calculate the checks. They can make customers either happy or dissatisfied.

Bus persons clean away soiled dishes and reset tables with fresh linen and silverware. They may also help clean up in the kitchen.

The work of sanitation and maintenance employees is essential. Although most dishwashing is done by machine, cooking equipment is washed by hand. Keeping walls and floors clean is always important.

Employers

Food service personnel are employed in restaurants of all kinds—coffee shops, fast-food chains, carryout operations cafeterias, store counters, department store tearooms, themed or entertainment restaurants, and "white tablecloth" facilities.

Food service is sometimes an integral part of a larger business such as a hotel, motel, club, factory, or corporation. Institutions such as schools, colleges, hospitals, the military service, nursing and convalescent homes, retirement centers, and prisons all maintain food service departments. Catering firms, vending machines, mobile trucks, and banquet and party contractors are also part of the food service industry.

Training

The food service industry provides one of the most extensive career ladders. It is possible to start at minimum wage or less; it is also possible to start without any special training. Top positions include some of the best-paid professionals and people with Ph.D. degrees.

Teenagers often get part-time jobs in fast-food establishments during high school and continue to increase both their experience and training as they climb the career ladder. Vocational high schools and community colleges offer the beginning training courses that lead to diplomas and associate degrees. At the completion of the two-year degree, it is not unusual to be offered an assistant manager's position. Some of the restaurant chains provide their own system of management training and prefer to start potential managers at minimal salaries and academic background. If these potential managers are competent, dependable, and hard working, and if they continue to increase their skills as well as their professionalism, there is no limit to their career possibilities.

Other people aspiring to food service careers will spend more time at the beginning at colleges and at universities. In 1996, more than 160 colleges and universities offered four-year programs in restaurant or institutional food service management. Most universities granting associate, bachelor's, and higher degrees provide on-the-job training as a part of required courses. It is possible to get enough experience during one's education to enter the career ladder at the management level. People with more academic training usually climb the ladder faster than those with less schooling.

Every state has community colleges, technical schools, and universities offering a variety of institutional and food service training programs. The state restaurant association in all states will provide a list of names and addresses for information. The state hotel and motel association is another source of information.

JOB OUTLOOK

Employment in the hospitality industry should grow about as fast as the average for all occupations through the year 2006. This is a field with a large amount of turnover, creating a great deal of opportunity for motivated new entrants into the job market. Hotel and motel managers, however, will face tough competition for the better jobs, as the number of managerial positions is expected to be reduced through consolidation, as more and more hotels and motels become part of larger corporate chains.

In the world of restaurant management, the job opportunities will be best for applicants with a bachelor's or associate degree in restaurant and institutional food management. Overall, restaurant jobs are expected to increase tremendously through the first decade of the twenty-first century, particularly in areas with increased populations and personal incomes. As well, the increasing percentage of elderly in the American population will lead to a steady demand for institutional managers.

SALARIES

There is a vast range of salaries within the institutional management profession, depending on one's place of employment and responsibilities. A survey by the National Restaurant Association revealed that the median base salary of restaurant managers was about $30,000 in 1995, although those at larger restaurants or institutional food service facilities earned more than $50,000. Beginning salaries for management trainees or assistant managers may be as low as $20,000 annually, even for people with college degrees.

Beginning salaries in larger organizations run from $21,000 to $30,000 annually. As years of experience, demonstrated competencies, and advanced training increase, so do opportunities to change positions or locations and to increase earnings. Executive chefs had a median base salary of $35,000 in 1995. It is not unusual for top administrators to make in excess of $60,000.

PROFESSIONAL ORGANIZATIONS

To learn more about careers in the hospitality industry, contact The American Hotel and Motel Association (AH&MA), Information Center, 1201 New York Avenue NW, Washington, DC 20005-3931.

Educational information is available for those interested in hotel and restaurant management by writing to the Council on Hotel, Restaurant, and Institutional Education, 1200 Seventeenth Street NW, Washington, DC 20036-3097.

Other useful professional organizations include the National Restaurant Association, 1200 Seventeenth Street NW, Washington, DC 20036-3097. Write the NRA for a directory of educational opportunities.

PROFILE: BED AND BREAKFAST MANAGER

Bed and breakfast operations are relatively new in Edith's state. In fact, her B&B was only the second one to be listed in the directory. Edith is head of the economics department of a large high school and expects to retire after three more years.

She grew up in the house that she turned into a limited country inn. Her father died when she was two, and she and her mother came to live with her grandparents on the farm that had been her great grandparents'. Her mother took a position as a secretary in a small city just three miles away, so Edith spent a lot of time with her grandparents and other relatives who came to visit for holidays, vacations, and weekends in the big farmhouse. She loved all the stories about the way life was lived there in pioneer days.

A college romance interrupted her plans to become a fashion director. She married at the end of her junior year in college and took a job to support her daughter Pam who was born during the second year of the marriage. Then her young husband died of a rare disease.

Like her mother, Edith came home to the big farmhouse with her baby, but she decided to complete her degree. A major university is located just thirty-five miles away. As a commuting student she earned a home economics teaching certificate in one and a half more years.

Edith began her teaching career in another state, and Pam went to nursery school while she taught. When they were home on summer vacation, the year Pam was ten, Edith learned of the home economics opening at the school where she now teaches, twenty-five miles from the farm. She and Pam lived in an apartment near the school until Pam went to college. At that time it seemed wise for Edith to again move back to the farmhouse with her mother and grandmother. Now Edith is alone in the house since her mother's death.

Over the years Edith and a friend have enjoyed vacationing in New England, where staying at bed and breakfast inns was a most enjoyable part of the trips that involved their interest in antiques.

The farmhouse has had numerous remodelings and modernization, but it still has its original lines and it appears to be just what it is—102 years old. Some of the furnishings have been around almost as long, and Edith is familiar with the history of them all, most dating back seventy-five years or more. When she supervised the latest addition to the house and kitchen, she checked out standards for a bed and breakfast license and made sure she could comply if she ever wanted to start the business.

Edith's sense of management told her that the house was an excellent resource for her later years. She would be surrounded by the things that would bring her pleasure and she would be able to entertain friends and family. She had the ability to organize and operate a small business and the location of the house was excellent. Business travelers at the nearby county seat often prefer "country hospitality." The college football games fill all the motels for fifty miles around on autumn weekends. The listing in the phone directory also would bring some cross-country business.

The business has grown as fast as Edith would let it. She has made sure that zoning regulations and local business rules are not violated. Now she accepts paying guests only during the summer and on football weekends. She rents the two upstairs bedrooms and makes available a continental-type breakfast.

Her price is $50.00 for a single room and $60.00 for a double. So far, expenses for the upkeep and changes in the house have served as excellent income tax deductions. An added pleasure is to tell visitors about the place and the antiques. Edith says this may become a more valuable compensation if she should get lonely after retirement.

PROFILE: TOURISM COORDINATOR

Beverly was not absolutely certain that she wanted a hotel restaurant career when she enrolled in the program at the start of her college life. She just wanted to be a student at her parents' alma mater, and that option seemed as good as any. In fact she was a bit surprised at how much she really liked her classes and her teachers.

During the summer after her sophomore year, she was employed for six weeks helping out at the chamber of commerce with the Blueberry Festival. It was a lot of fun making radio and TV appearances, getting stories and pictures in the papers, arranging for a pie contest and a children's blueberry-picking contest, and helping local civic and church organizations set up booths around the town square for the weekend. The Saturday night of the festival included a presentation of the blueberry queen, a band concert, street dancing, and lots of eating. She put in many hours but felt rewarded because the entire event was so successful. Little did she realize that it would lead to a full-time position and maybe her life's career.

The State Bureau of Tourism employs some college students during the summers, and after Beverly's junior year she accepted one of these positions. She used her experience and the ideas she had learned in classes to assist festival committees in the entire southwestern corner of her state. She enjoyed traveling around to the various communities, learning about their special events and helping them to become successful in attracting visitors who would spend money.

The appointment to a full-time more or less permanent position in the bureau became a possibility during Beverly's second summer as temporary help. She knew the opening was likely to be available and that her uncle's political clout might help her get the appointment, so she delayed looking for other positions.

Beverly now has more office work to do than in the summer jobs and her territory is the entire state. She has been asked to especially promote and assist with ethnic festivals in the northern industrial cities of her state.

Beverly knows that patronage positions can be lost as quickly as they are gained, but she believes that the contacts she makes will be very valuable. If her work results in profitable festivals, she can easily find another employer. Her salary is $20,000 plus her expenses while traveling, and she says that no one can have more fun on the job.

SUGGESTED ADDITIONAL READING

Medlik, S. *The Business of Hotels.* New York: Butterworth-Heinemann, 1995.

Rue, Nancy N. *Choosing a Career in Hotels, Motels, and Resorts.* New York: Rosen Publishing Group, 1996.

Rutherford, Denney G. (editor). *Hotel Management and Operations.* New York: John Wiley and Sons, 1997.

CHAPTER 9

HOME ECONOMICS EDUCATION

More home economists choose to work in education than in any other field. Opportunities in education range from being a teacher in an elementary, junior high, or high school, to working as a cooperative extension instructor, to being employed by organizations and local governments to offer courses to community residents. Home economists often begin their careers as instructors before moving on to a specialized role as a dietitian, interior designer, or other related field.

Trained home economics teachers play an interesting role in our nation's schools. In the past, the subject was usually associated with teaching young women how to manage certain household tasks. Now the goal of the curriculum is much broader and is equally aimed at boys. Home economics education helps students learn how to interpret and understand family and work life. As society goes through changes, so does the home economics curriculum. The social, economic, and technological changes that both young people and adults face are proper topics for home economics instruction. By learning how to manage family resources effectively, purchase and consume foods and other consumer goods wisely, and nurture and care for others, the home economics instructor is contributing to the students' general ability to function in the society.

The home and the family have always been a basic institution in American life. When the family system does not function, other problems—such as malnutrition, teenage pregnancy, child abuse, and consumer fraud—are intensified. Most values and habits relating to everyday living are learned informally in the family setting. Thus, examining family issues and relationships in a school setting, and encouraging clear thinking on the various roles and influences of family life, is very beneficial to young people.

REMOVING THE GENDER BARRIER

Learning how to cope with family, work, and social situations is a proper course of study for both male and female students. The number of males enrolled in the home economics curriculum has increased primarily because when a course is required in the public schools, it can no longer be required only for females. Attitudes and appreciations as well as skills involved in satisfying home living can be learned at school. This is especially important for students coming from single-parent homes, families with both parents working full-time, and for only-children. These are situations that are common in today's society.

The number of home economics courses required by states and local school boards is usually limited to the junior high level and possibly one course in high school. The curriculum of home economics includes foods and nutrition, consumer education, home management, parenting, independent living, clothing and textiles, family living, child development, interior design, home furnishings and applied art, and home economics related occupations. Most teachers below the college level must be able to teach more than one of these subject matter areas.

Good teachers must know what to teach and how to teach it. The competencies required include the ability to do each of the following:

- assess the needs of the people to be served through working with advisory committees, conducting surveys, and making home and family contacts;
- comprehend the principles and philosophy of vocational education;
- relate legislative program purposes to specific needs of the community;
- integrate the subject matter areas of home economics as they relate to the occupation of homemaking;
- demonstrate essential skills required by the occupation of homemaking or for specific occupations related to home economics;
- direct out-of-class experiences for individual students that relate to appropriate aspects of the occupation; and

- integrate the activities of FHA/HERO (Future Home-makers of America/Home Economics Related Occupations clubs) with the total vocational home economics program to achieve the overall objectives.

Basic preparation in home economics subject matter and educational techniques are the foundations of good teaching. In preparing for a career teaching home economics, one generally takes classes in such areas as Individual and Family Development, Contemporary Issues in Food and Nutrition, and Consumer Issues and Problems. (See Appendix C for sample courses of study for home economics teaching.)

Home economics education can be general or vocational. The choice as to whether one or both curricula are taught is dependent on the local school administration. Its decision may depend upon the way the needs of the community are viewed; the decision also is influenced by the availability of state and federal funds. Legislation that provides federal funds is fairly specific about how these funds are used. The vocational curriculum is divided into consumer homemaking and cooperative occupational programs. Many subject matter courses will qualify in both programs. The subject matter content of the cooperative occupational program is related to work experience. HERO clubs are a vital part of the occupational program. They offer students the opportunity to develop leadership skills, explore career paths, and interact with the community. Teachers in the cooperative occupational program need to be skilled in public relations and in working with employers. In high schools a substantial amount of their time is used outside the classroom involving longer hours than for most teachers.

Home economists who administer educational programs must keep up-to-date, envision the future, carry responsibility, and relate the significance of their programs to the decision makers. School home economics programs offer excellent opportunities for professional public relations—almost every voter has a child, or a grandchild, or a friend or neighbor who expresses an opinion about the quality of their home economics courses and the relevance of those courses to everyday life.

COOPERATIVE EXTENSION PROGRAMS

Most cooperative extension positions are funded by federal, state, and local sources. The federal appropriation is a part of the budget of the Department of Agriculture. Both the state and federal monies are administered by the land grant colleges. Local (usually county) funds are controlled in a cooperative way at the state level with the county officials.

The need for home economists was demonstrated early in the development of educational program for farm families. The first county extension offices were established prior to World War I to encourage farmers to use the knowledge developed at the agricultural experiment stations. The effectiveness of the education was measured in the productivity of the farm. Extension agents soon found that adopted practices were dependent upon convincing farmers of the value of modern technology. Soon 4-H Clubs were initiated as a way of reaching farm families. The farm business was a family business. It was impossible to separate the welfare of the farm family from the profitability of the farm business.

Early extension home economists organized homemaker groups as a way of dispersing information. Home economists from land grant colleges held educational sessions and developed instructional material for local leaders to share with their neighborhood clubs or organizations. This effective method continues today.

Extension specialists in all phases of home economics are a part of the land grant college staff. Some hold joint appointments between extension and university teaching or extension and research. Extension specialists educate the community on topics ranging from best agricultural and dairy practices to household economics, natural resource management and recycling, and maintaining clean soil and water.

Most extension home economists are county based. Their offices, secretary, mileage, and supplies are provided by their base county. They carry the responsibility for the organization and the public relations for the home economics programs in their counties. They must be well-informed generalists and often at the same time specialists in one or more of the home economics phases. Within a region they share teaching responsibility in several counties.

Extension programs, although never exclusively directed to the farm population, increasingly emphasize serving the entire population with informational programs on food and nutrition, parenting, and family relations. Especially in the more urban counties, agents use the mass media to reach their constituents. The informality of extension methods has contributed greatly to success in changing the lives of those less privileged.

An important phase of extension is the youth program, of which 4-H is the largest and the best known. Home economists who work in these programs assist leaders with projects for the youth such as nutrition, food preservation, crafts, child care, and so on. A substantial amount of the professional's job involves recruiting volunteer leaders, arranging for recognition for members' work well done, and developing leadership among the youth. Providing learning opportunities at exhibits at county and state fairs and in camp settings are effective methods.

EDUCATION REQUIRED

Positions at most middle and high schools and county cooperative extensions are available to beginning home economists with a bachelor's degree. Employers expect educators to constantly upgrade their qualifications. Home economists may choose to do their graduate work in one phase of home economics or a subject-matter area connected with their profession, such as business, education, or journalism.

Higher education institutions offering advanced degrees in home economics conduct much basic research. Students enrolled in graduate programs contribute to the effort. University faculties not only teach classes but plan, organize, and supervise research projects.

PROFESSIONAL ORGANIZATIONS

Professional organizations include the American Association of Family and Consumer Sciences, its state and district affiliates, the American Vocational Association, the American Federation of Teachers and its affiliates, and the National Education Association and its state affiliates. The more populous counties have local organizations of home economists.

SALARIES

Beginning salaries range from $18,000 to $25,000 a year. In most public schools, teachers contract for their positions as part of an organized group that negotiates the wage scale. As the education qualifications and number of years of experience increase, so do salaries. There is a trend toward modifying these scales to include the evaluation of a teacher's performance. Teachers with substantial training beyond the master's degree plus ten or more years of experience will get up to $40,000 per year. Although extension personnel do not have negotiated contracts, their salaries are comparable. Salaries in higher education and administration may exceed these standards.

PROFILE: VOCATION EDUCATION COORDINATOR

Lee had five years of teaching experience when he was offered the position of coordinator of occupational education in home economics. One consideration influencing his decision to accept the position was that it would allow him the time for the personal satisfaction he enjoys in the accomplishments of his students.

The compensation for an occupational education coordinator for his school is more than for a teacher. The salary would be two hundred dollars a month more than the regular schedule. For Lee this would be an eleven-month contract rather than a regular school-year contract. Although he would be reimbursed for most of his expenses, there would be some tax advantage in nonreimbursed car ownership expenses.

Lee believes that the additional community involvement would be an advantage for him. He enjoys activities such as visiting and locating training stations, writing articles for the newspaper, being a guest on a radio talk show, and planning community programs.

The added responsibility and hours of work would be a definite disadvantage for some people because as a coordinator one would seldom be free in the late afternoon, and a summer job would be impossible. Lee would be responsible for being out of town attending conferences probably six to ten days per year. For some people this would interfere too much with home responsibilities.

Lee is attracted to this position because of the relationship he would develop with the students. Many high school students respond to learning situations in the real world more favorably than in the academic setting. A start on the career ladder often encourages students to continue learning new skills and increase their competencies. Association with those working in the marketplace motivates students to become more valuable employees by developing promptness, pleasant manners, and courtesy with customers. Students appreciate the opportunity to earn money while in school, and for some this is the first time they have felt successful. Some students continue as full-time workers after graduation with the employers, grow on the job, and are eternally grateful. Lee realizes that for him the satisfaction of seeing students develop in this way would be a benefit that he could not measure.

At the school Lee would not only consult with students but conduct classes. He is aware of the students' other classes and would make his class as relevant as possible to their work experience. He would use his experience from visiting students on the job in planning class discussion. He would also arrange for guest speakers.

Lee believes that he would find it challenging to work with employers in developing the jobs in which his students would be placed and to evaluate their progress both personally and vocationally.

PROFILE: FOODS AND NUTRITION TEACHER

Sharon could not have been more pleased with her student teaching experience. She taught foods and nutrition—her favorite subjects—with a well-known, excellent teacher who was head of the home economics department in a large high school near the university. Her enthusiastic and thorough work was noticed, and Sharon was selected to fill a position teaching foods in the adjoining junior high school upon her graduation.

During her first year of teaching, Sharon attended a Home Economics Association meeting and heard about a special program that was being proposed for pregnant students. She volunteered to help work out courses in home economics subjects, especially nutrition and child development. It was quite a challenge, but her mentor from student teaching days was a big help, and so were her professors at the university.

The following year the program was begun with a total of fifteen students. Sharon taught the food and nutrition section and found the experience very satisfying. The students were surely at risk nutritionally because of poor diets, their own adolescent needs, and the needs of their unborn babies. Both mental and physical handicaps often can be traced to immature mothers and poor nutrition during the prenatal period. An example would be for the adolescent mother to drink sodas and munch potato chips rather than eat well-balanced meals. The value of the program was appreciated by the school administration, and it has continued ever since.

Sharon has completed her master's degree and has a specialty in the child development area. She participated in several conferences on the issue of teenage pregnancy and developed programs that she used at school. Some of these she continues to use now that she teaches in this program full-time. There is good evidence that the program makes a real difference in the lives of the students. They learn to appreciate the importance of family life, to plan parenthood, and to use contraceptives.

Her salary and fringe benefits are on the same schedule as all the other teachers in the system.

PROFILE: EXTENSION SPECIALIST

Warren is an extension specialist in family life in the state where he finished his Ph.D. earlier this year. He took the position while still a student with the understanding that he would complete his graduate work and would adjust his schedule in order to accomplish that goal.

He was invited to apply for the position because he was doing research in the area of family stress—particularly the ways financial stress affects husband-wife and parent-child relationships. Two county extension home economists, one in a rural and one in an urban county, had helped him to arrange interviews with 122 families to gather data on just how they had coped with financial crises and what they believed had been the results on their relationships.

The associate dean, who is Warren's immediate superior, decided to add at least a half-time specialist position in family life to her staff when the farm crisis in her state brought on a large increase in foreclosures. Many agents in counties were asking for help in setting up programs to assist families with heavy debt loads and reduced incomes. There had been at least six suicides related to foreclosures, many divorces, and incidents of runaway children. Now the second family life position is full-time because of the demand from both urban and farm counties for programs related to family stress. The department now has one less clothing specialist than it did three years ago.

Warren shares office space and a secretary with the other family life specialist on the campus of a land grant university that has 21,000 students and a total staff of 8,500. He likes the stimulation of his setting and the association with research workers and graduate students. He is part of the sixteen-member university-based home economics extension staff that works with 254 extension agents based in the counties of the state. Most of his programs are arranged by the 73 home economics agents, but increasingly youth, agriculture, and community development agents ask for his assistance.

About 65 percent of his time is spent on campus planning and preparing for programs and producing literature and media material that can be used by agents or distributed as handouts. The other 35 percent of Warren's time is used in the counties working directly with agents. Last month he adjusted his schedule in order to help in a county that just learned that a major heavy industry employer was planning to close a plant and lay off three thousand workers. He has also become involved with regional training programs of leaders of support groups for families of alcoholics.

SUGGESTED ADDITIONAL READING

Kimbrell, Grady. *Personal and Family Economics.* Florence, KY: West Pub., 1995.

Parnell, Frances B. and Joyce H. Wooten. *Skills for Living.* Chicago, IL: Goodheart, 1997.

CHAPTER 10

FAMILY ECONOMICS
AND FINANCIAL PLANNING

Families and individuals often need assistance in learning how to effectively manage their household finances. Careful planning and clear goals help people in their efforts to achieve greater stability and happiness. The role of home economists who specialize in family economics and home management is quite distinct from the role of financial planning in the business world. In a family situation, the goals are not as easily defined—the purpose is not to maximize profit, but to create a harmonious system in which every member of the family benefits.

Another unique aspect of family economics and home management is the nature of the resources. Whereas businesses measure the cost of labor and the dollar value of goods and services, a family's resources includes the time, energy, education, and aptitudes of the household members. Moreover, there is a *real* value to a family in spending time on activities that enhance the happiness of each family member, whether it is reading to a child at night or keeping an orderly house and providing healthy, nutritious meals.

Family economists are particularly sensitive to the various capabilities of every individual.

FINANCIAL COUNSELING

High school home economics classes provide students with a solid foundation on consumer education, focusing on areas such as shopping skills. Comparative shopping, studies in advertising, and record keeping can save an educated consumer as much as 30 percent in the cost of items purchased or can make it possible to increase one's level of consumption an equal amount. Some states require the completion of courses aimed at developing these skills before students can graduate from high school.

Some financial organizations such as banks, savings and loans, and insurance companies employ home economists. Indeed, recent shifts in our economy are bringing rapid growth in the family service industries. Assertive family economists will be able to develop positions within the financial industry in the coming century. Functions of home economists in financial organizations include preparing educational material, serving as counselors for clients, training staff members, consulting with management, and promoting the image of their company as one serving family interests.

Helping families plan for financial security is a very important part of financial counseling. This involves an understanding of insurance, pension plans, taxes, investments in stocks and bonds, and real estate.

Some universities offer financial counseling as a specific option in their home economics colleges or consumer and family science programs. Most financial counselors assisting clients with investments are affiliated with corporations that sell insurance, mutual funds, or stocks and bonds or all of these. Usually compensation involves working for commissions.

To maintain the ethical standards of a professional home economist and compete with other salespeople in the financial area requires a great deal of maturity. There is a growing pressure in the marketplace for the regulation of financial planners.

The establishment and rapid growth of the International Association of Financial Planning is a response attempt at self regulation within the profession. The designation of Certified Financial Planner is now given to graduates of the College of Financial Planning. An effort is now being made to get government regulation similar to that of stock brokers and real estate agents, for financial planners.

As investments become more complex and as an individual's available time is more scarce, the investment counselor's service is in growing demand.

For more information about careers as a family financial planner, contact the International Association of Financial Planning, Suite B-300, 5775 Glenridge Drive NE, Atlanta, GA 30328-5364. The Internet address is www.iafp.org.

REAL ESTATE AGENTS

Licensed real estate agents who are also home economists are exceptionally qualified to work as salespeople in the housing market because of their unique understanding of the housing needs of families.When consumers consider buying residential property they consider both their housing and investment needs. Compensation in this area is a matter of sales commissions. It is possible to put in long hours and earn more than the average income. It is also possible to work only on weekends.

CONSUMER CREDIT SPECIALISTS

Assisting families with consumer credit has been a specialized part of the home economics profession for nearly fifty years. As of 1999, there were more than 1,450 counseling centers. These nonprofit agencies provide money management education, credit and debt counseling, and other services to individuals and families.

Counselors typically spend one-and-one-half to two hours with an individual or a couple. This is an opportunity to get acquainted with the expenses involved in their lifestyle, the extent of their indebtedness, and the sources, amounts, and frequency of their income. Most of the clients have overextended their use of credit and are seeking help to get their budgets back in balance. Reduced income, illness, and divorce are most often the reasons for clients' problems.

Most financial companies and issuers of credit cards participate in the National Foundation for Consumer Credit (NFCC) and cooperate with counselors. They do this by agreeing to temporarily accept reduced monthly payments while clients work with the counselor to get their debts under control. These agencies are not-for-profit organizations and are authorized to operate a trust fund into which clients make deposits and from which checks are mailed to their creditors.

Occasionally banks, finance companies, and credit unions offer similar services. Wage earner plans that are supervised by the courts (Bankruptcy Chapter 13) provide protection to consumers while they work out a debt repayment plan. Serving as a trustee in these programs is an appropriate position for a home economist.

To find out more about the NFCC, write to the National Foundation for Consumer Credit, 8611 Second Avenue, Silver Spring, MD 20910. The Internet address is www.nfcc.org.

CONSUMER AFFAIRS

In the early 1960s, during the administration of President John Kennedy, the consumer came to the forefront of public attention. Kennedy's declaration of consumer rights included the right to information, the right to safety, the right to choose, and the right to be heard.

Home economists employed in consumer affairs sometimes work in a department of the government such as the Food and Drug Administration, the Department of Weights and Measures, or the Bureau of Standards. The Federal Trade

Commission (FTC) is the government organization that enforces a variety of antitrust and consumer protection laws. The FTC also houses the Bureau of Consumer Protection.

Home economists are to be found at consumer affairs offices that have been established or enlarged at national, state, and local levels. Responsibilities include enforcing the law on labels, advertising, and warranties. At the national level product standards are developed. There are standards for food products such as the amount of fat in hot dogs, the difference between salad dressing and mayonnaise, the sizes of pans, the weights of motor oil, the heights of kitchen cabinets, and so on.

In some positions the consumer affairs professional spends most of the time in the laboratory, and in others the professional is in the marketplace checking on products or on manufacturing processes.

Private organizations or corporations employ consumer specialists to do testing, write brochures, field press inquires, and lobby Congress.

An important part of the professional's job is to respond to consumer complaints. Sometimes this is a simple matter of informal arbitration, and sometimes this requires court action.

Consumer and family law is a good area of study for a graduate home economist. Building an understanding of family issues is a natural for someone in home economics. Home economists function well in this graduate specialization.

INDEPENDENT HOUSEKEEPING AGENCIES

One growing area of business is in the field of owner-operated agencies that supply housekeeping services. An interesting example was reported in a news article telling of two home economists having lunch one day and brainstorming possible self-employment businesses. One of them wondered who took care of the apartments in the John Hancock Building, a high-rise in Chicago. After investigating and receiving approval from the building management, they delivered leaflets advertising their services under each apartment door. The response to their leaflets convinced them that the demand for a dependable housekeeping service was worthy of establishing such a business. They performed and experimented until they had standardized the procedure and equipment needed in the cleaning of the apartments. They then hired and trained employees to perform these services. The demand for their services and their skillful management made their company a successful expanded corporation.

More information on this potentially lucrative career direction can be obtained by contacting the International Executive Housekeepers Association, Inc., 1001 Eastwind Drive, Suite 301, Westerville, OH 43081-3361. The Internet address is ieha.org.

PROFILE: CONSUMER CREDIT COUNSELOR

Glen has been working in his first professional position for six months and is delighted with his work and lifestyle. He graduated with a family economics home management major at the land grant college of his home state. Two weeks later he began as a counselor at the consumer credit counseling service in the city where the state capital is located.

He finds great satisfaction in knowing that more than half of the individuals and couples get on a debt repayment program and work themselves into a comfortable and secure situation while learning to control the flow of cash through their family budget. His office hours are from 9:00 A.M. to 5:00 P.M. three days a week and from 11:00 A.M. to 8:00 P.M. two days a week. He expects to take the certification test for credit counselors when it is given at the annual meeting of the National Foundation for Consumer Credit next fall.

The feeling of independence that has come with being able to pay for his own small apartment near his office in the city's downtown area as well as beginning repayment on his college loan is wonderful. He has enough money to enjoy plays, concerts, and restaurants at least once a week at his beginning salary of $15,000. His first raise should come in about a month.

He has joined an organization of social workers that meets for lunch for professional reasons and a citywide singles group at the church of his denomination for personal reasons. He may start graduate work a little later in either law or social welfare. But for now, it is great to be a young urban professional contributing to the economic and family welfare of his community and to be expecting an even brighter future.

SUGGESTED ADDITIONAL READING

Katz, Phyllis A. and Margaret Katz. *The Feminist Dollar: The Wise Woman's Buying Guide.* New York: Plenum Press, 1997.
Taylor, Binah Breet. *Buyer Beware: Safeguarding Consumer Rights.* Philadelphia: Rourke Book Co., 1997.

CHAPTER 11

FASHION DESIGN AND MERCHANDISING

The world of fashion is one of inspiration, glamour, and high society. In movies such as the documentary *Unzipped,* about the cutting-edge fashion designer Isaac Mizrahi, and the fictional *Ready-To-Wear,* we also are treated to the intrigue and competition of this unique industry. Fashion is a specialization that appeals to many future home economists. While many are drawn to the high gloss of the couture world, which serves a small and elite cadre of international socialites, far more seek careers in the design, production, distribution, and marketing of clothing and accessories to men, women, and children of all incomes.

Careers in fashion come in three "styles": those dealing with design, those involved with production, and the wide range of jobs that make up the world of merchandising. The designers create the styles and patterns for clothing and accessories. They can make fashion news by coming up with a new "line," or by employing colors, fabric, and fit in a novel way. Others find a niche, such as serving working women or creating clothing that is appropriate for casual lifestyles.

Jobs in the clothing production industry begin with duplicating the original design and continue through finishing the completed item of clothing. Then the merchandising machine takes over, distributing the clothes to the retailers where the satisfied consumer can purchase them.

Home economists have always been concerned with the family's clothing. This concern includes the quality and cost of garments themselves, their care, upkeep, and safety, as well as the psychological and sociological effect on the lifestyle of the wearer. Prior to the twentieth century, clothing was produced at home for most families. As the apparel industry has grown, home economists have made professional contributions and have created careers that integrate the specialized needs and interests of the industry with their concerns for the well-being of the individual and the family.

DESIGN

Fashion has been a mode of personal and cultural expression from days of our earliest ancestors. As we enter the twenty-first century it is a very international industry. Clothing may be designed in one country, assembled in another, and then sold around the world.

The design world demands quite a lot of preparation from its practitioners. Most students entering the textile design field will need at least two years of training for positions such as textile artist, colorist, assistant to stylist, knit and embroidery designer, hand weaver, and silk screen artist. Most positions require someone who is creative and has a good sense of color as well as a feeling for and understanding of the environment in which the product will be used. For example, conservation of energy helps to popularize woolens, sweaters, or jackets. With more women working, fabrics suitable for tailored suits are in demand. Easy care is an important factor in the clothing of children. Textile designers are usually employed by fabric producers.

Apparel designers create new styles for men's, women's, and children's clothing and accessories. The trends are established by a few well-known designers in cities like Paris, Rome, New York, Dallas, and Los Angeles. Most positions of apparel designers are with manufacturers of ready-to-wear. The designers who work with a company must work within the limitations of the market that the manufacturer wants to satisfy. For example, some manufacturers produce apparel for a very special price range and, in some cases, for an age range. Others work in only one type of garment, such as sportswear. A small percentage of designers work on a freelance basis.

In a typical design room, there is probably a head designer with one or two assistants. A designer must have a knowledge of fabrics, trimmings, color, construction processes, and costs. Designers obtain ideas visiting art galleries and museums and by keeping up to date with magazines and newspapers. Sometimes they get their ideas from available fabrics and accessories. They spend a great deal of their time sketching. They may have assistants who complete sketches of their ideas. Sometimes the designer actually works with the fabric and drapes the garment on a mannequin, although this is often assigned to an assistant. This is a very competitive field of work. One designer who we talked with was expected to sketch twenty-five designs a week. Of course, only a few of these designs ever enter final production and become garments.

PRODUCTION

In the large firms there will be a production manager who oversees the work from the design room to the sales representatives. In small firms the general manager may oversee all of these operations, including patternmaking, layout, cutting, and assembly through actual sewing, pressing, and packaging. The manager or the assistant will keep records of merchandise produced, inventory control, and shipping records. These records expedite work flow and deliveries. A profile in apparel design production indicates that entry-level jobs may lead to more complex careers, depending on the attitudes and interests of the workers.

MERCHANDISING

The market is the meeting of buyers and sellers. The manufacturers of apparel maintain showrooms for this purpose.

During certain seasons they may rent additional space in showroom centers; they also have salespeople who travel making visits to retail establishments. Many times the manufacturers produce appropriate sales promotion materials, which they either give or sell to their retail level customers.

The fashion director or buyer is a merchandiser who works as part of the merchandising team and makes merchandising decisions. The fashion director's responsibilities will vary from one store to another.

The director's responsibility is to see that the department is up to date with fashion trends. To some extent the director is a trendsetter for his or her particular clientele. In some cases the fashion director is the buyer, while in other cases the assistants do the buying. In the day-to-day routine the responsibilities include reading journals and magazine releases, attending fashion presentations, and taking part in many meetings. The fashion director makes many phone calls and returns phone calls. He or she may direct style shows and handle market research, special events, and youth activities.

The fashion director needs to look the part, have communication skills, and be sensitive to the reactions of others. This is a position that requires a lot of stamina and a willingness to work irregular and sometimes very long hours.

A very important function of the fashion director is to train the personnel in the store, including salespeople, the buyers, the assistant managers, and the advertising people. Often a most important function of the fashion director is interpreting her or his ideas to the company management.

The positions under the fashion director will vary according to the store. The assistant managers and buyers may be allocated according to types of merchandise—that is, lingerie, dresses, suits, coats, sportswear, and accessories. In a large department store the buyer's responsibility may be even more narrow, such as women's dresses in the moderate price range.

Buyers are frequently given a budget for a season. They must decide what to buy and from which manufacturers to buy. They will contact the wholesaler and agree on the price and delivery date. At the store the buyer sets the price at which the item will be offered and supervises the stockroom and the sales staff. The buyers will help promote, display, and advertise. They decide the appropriate time for reducing the price and recommend the amount of the reduction.

EDUCATION AND TRAINING

Fashion design and production is taught at community colleges and four-year colleges as well as at specialized fashion and art and design institutions. The students take courses and participate in an internship or an apprenticeship as a part of their training.

Without formal education from a post–high school institution, the beginning salesperson has an opportunity to learn the stock, to sell, and to build clientele. However, the student with a two-year or four-year degree will advance more rapidly than the individual without a college background.

SALARY

The range in fashion careers goes from the salesclerk to top management. Success is dependent upon talent, training, and hard work. Expertise in merchandising for the home economists can easily be shifted from fashions to interiors or any consumer-related product. A variety of retail experience provides a way to enter top management. Financial rewards vary with the initiative of the individual, the amount of responsibility, and the degree to which he or she is able to provide leadership within the corporation and within the community of the clientele.

Beginning jobs are usually at minimum wage. The individual may advance with initiative, training, diligence, and formal education. There are many part-time positions that offer an opportunity to combine learning and work but may have the disadvantage of low pay and few benefits. It is reasonable for a four-year college graduate to expect to earn $25,000 to $35,000 annually after five years of experience. There is no limit to top salaries for those who move up the corporate ladder.

JOB OUTLOOK

Employment opportunities in design are expected to grow faster than the average for all occupations. Demand for fashion and textile designers should increase as consumers earn more and become increasingly concerned with fashion and style.

The fashion business is one in which small boutiques flourish. Opportunities for entrepreneurship can include operating specialty fabric shops, weaving, providing alterations, dressmaking, and working as a consultant.

PROFESSIONAL ORGANIZATIONS

There are numerous professional and consumer organizations dedicated to the fashion industry. One good organization to start with is The Fashion Group International, which was founded in 1931. This is a nonprofit professional organization with more than 6,000 members in the fashion industry:

Fashion Group International
    597 Fifth Avenue, 8th Floor
    New York, NY 10017
    Internet address: www.fga.org

Another professional organization involved in the fashion industry is:

The American Association of Textile Chemists and Colorists
    One Davis Drive, P.O. Box 12215
    Research Triangle Park, NC 27709-2215
    Internet address: www.aatcc.org

PROFILE: DRESS BROKER

For Jody the "almost new" clothing shops were an intriguing and completely new experience on a field trip

during her junior year in college. Her only ideas of marketing used clothing had been gained by browsing at rummage
sales or by making gifts to the Salvation Army. Here she
saw and touched labels like Bill Blass, Ralph Lauren, Carl
Lagerfeld, Willi Smith, Giorgio Saint Angelo, Albert Nipon,
Perry Ellis, Betsey Johnson, and Oscar de la Renta on garments that appeared to have never been worn. Although the
shop itself was just a "hole in the wall," the merchandise
reeked of elegance, and it was just a half block off a boule-
vard known as the Magnificent Mile; Jody's dream career
was cast. She wanted to broker expensive dresses, suits,
coats, and sportswear that society women had worn once or
twice and were selling.

Her mentor was able to help her get a list of names and
addresses of such shops, and she wrote to all of them seeking summer employment. Her best offer was to work on
commission as an alteration lady in a shop in a large northern city. Although she barely earned enough money to
cover her expenses, she enjoyed the ten weeks and con-
firmed her desire to build a career in recycling designer
fashions.

In the fall of Jody's senior year, she again wrote to all the
resale shops that she had contacted in the spring and told of
her summer experience, her school program, and her desire
for a position after graduation.

She was thrilled with the offer of an interview by a
manager-owner who wanted to go away for the summer and
maybe begin retirement. The manager-owner had contacted

her employer of the preceeding summer and was pleased with the favorable recommendation. Although there were no guarantees, Jody was happy to take the challenge. She believed that she could earn enough to get by in the beginning and that she could prove her worth and ability.

Most garments were brought in by consignors. Jody inspected each item—it had to be clean, up-to-date, and of a quality appropriate for the shop's customers. The task of pricing required a lot of judgment. Of course the seller and the shop wanted to get as much as possible, but to make a profit, merchandise had to move quickly. Usually items were tagged at little more than one-third of the original price. If an item sold within thirty days, the shop kept 50 percent. During the second month the split was 60 percent for the shop and 40 percent for the consignor. At that point the consignor might take items home or leave them at the shop. If left, the items could stay on the half-price rack for another thirty days before being given to charity. Nothing stayed in the shop more than three months.

Jody often stayed late, doing the alteration work herself and completing the paperwork. Her diligence paid off. At the end of the summer, she had a small profit for the manager-owner and had doubled her own earnings, which were based on a one-third commission of the clothing she accepted, of the previous summer. The owner was impressed with Jody's success and is now offering her a partnership in the business.

PROFILE: FASHION MERCHANDISER

As a high school graduating senior, Rob decided he wanted to go into fashion merchandising. As he looked over universities in which to enroll in this home economics program, two of his criteria were, 1) the school must offer a degree in fashion merchandising, and 2) it must offer an internship during the junior or senior year. These programs are sometimes called work study or co-op programs. In the internship program he would have selling experience. It might include summer, vacation, and Christmas holidays time as well as the regular school term in New York. Rob expected this experience to give him a chance at hands-on learning about stock routines and merchandise.

During Rob's sophomore year he was able to get a part-time job in a large department store working on Saturdays and during the Christmas vacation. He gained much awareness of a fast-moving industry. He learned to work as a cashier, wrote up sales tickets, and handled refunds. During the Thanksgiving break he helped to arrange new merchandise on the shelf and set up counter displays.

During his junior year in New York, he was employed thirty-five hours a week at near minimum wage. He also was enrolled in two classes each semester. On the job he learned a lot about what to say and what not to say to customers as well as co-workers by observing the way seasoned salespeople successfully handled difficult situations. Rob knew that their commission was more important than their base salary.

Rob spent eight weeks in the receiving and marking room where he learned how to handle stock and how to keep inventory records. Another valuable part of his experience was his contact with buyers and assistant buyers. He became knowledgeable about the way they work with branch stores and with clerical people.

Now Rob is a senior who is enthusiastic, energetic, and confident that he is on his way in the fashion business. He dresses well and looks the part of a fashion expert. He is a "people person" and enjoys being around others. He expects to have the choice of several assistant buyer's positions at the end of the year. He has had his experience in the beginning jobs. He may move into executive training after his experience as a buyer.

PROFILE: TEXTILES CURATOR

Brenda has loved beautiful fabrics since she was a small girl and made what she thought were elegant costumes for her dolls. She realized after two years as a clothing and textile major in college that the modern fashion market was not an environment that she would enjoy. However, she has found the perfect position for herself—assistant to the director of the textiles division of a major natural history museum.

Her assignments have been varied. One assignment involved displaying the rugs and other ceremonial textiles that were part of a special three-month show from Northern India. Another involved laboratory efforts to clean and study material recovered from some South American archaeological digs. The research aspects of Brenda's position interest her the most. She has perfected a method of laundering ancient fabrics in such a way that they do not move. Even if they are in fragments, the original weave and design are preserved.

She seldom works outside regular daytime hours. The annual starting salary for a textiles curator is in the low $20,000 range, but she can expect regular increases if she performs well and continues updating her education. The museum personnel policy includes two weeks of paid vacation for professional staff and increases to four weeks after five years of service. She is provided with full health insurance and a pension plan in addition to social security. She has made friends with other staff members and looks forward to a long career.

SUGGESTED ADDITIONAL READING

Frings, Gini Stephen. *Fashion: From Concept to Consumer.* New York: Prentice Hall, 1999.

Mauro, Lucia. *Careers for Fashion Plates and Other Trendsetters.* Lincolnwood, IL: VGM Career Horizons, 1996.

Samuel, Wendy, et al. *Fashion Careers.* New York: Pocket Productions, 1999.

CHAPTER 12

AN EVOLVING AND DYNAMIC PROFESSION

Home economics as a profession is closely in touch with the changes in American society. The field initially developed at a time when America was shifting from an agricultural to an industrial economy. The goal of the early home economists was to improve the quality of family and work life in America by disseminating the most current information on health, nutrition, shelter, and other consumer issues.

Home economics continues to be a relevant field and has kept current with the more recent trend towards a high-tech, information- and service-oriented economy. As new developments occur in the fields of nutrition, for example, the home economists are on the forefront of helping to spread the news over better ways to maintain health. Similarly, as women have assumed a more equal footing in the work world, home economics responds to the new challenges, with increased emphasis on securing quality child care and other services for the new American family.

Because home economics is such a flexible field, the opportunities for new entrants will continue to blossom in the twenty-first century. The training opportunities for home economists have expanded to include far more technical challenges than in the past.

The role of the home economics professional now overlaps with a wide range of professions, including dietitians, educators, financial planners, and designers, to name just a few of the career paths discussed in the previous pages. It is possible for a person to enter the field with a specialization in one area, based on the general education received toward the accomplishment of a bachelor's degree, and then branch into other specializations with proper training and certification.

FINDING THE JOBS

Home economists are characteristically self-starters, highly motivated, goal oriented, risk takers, and versatile individuals. These attitudes coupled with training, skills, and experience make it possible for home economists to find or create a position wherein they may profitably practice their profession in almost any situation.

A professional home economist will actively keep up to date with new opportunities for the profession to serve the public. Ways of doing this are participating in professional organizations, reading professional magazines, attending conferences, and serving on committees. The American Association of Family and Consumer Sciences and its state and regional affiliates are active throughout the United State, providing opportunities to make connections and learn of available positions.

The creative home economist relates current events to his or her profession when listening to television news programs and reading newspapers and magazines. This may present the opportunity to volunteer expertise in some type of crisis. It may involve knowing the kind of decisions the local school board is making or knowing what kind of grants local governments are obtaining from outside sources. Knowing what is happening in the workplace of major employers may stimulate ideas for a contribution from home economics and the possibility of new job opportunities.

Being active in community organizations such as the Business and Professional Women's Club and serving on boards such as the Better Business Bureau and the Urban League create opportunities to relate the broad spectrum of the home economics profession to community action.

LIVING UP TO THE IMAGE

Home economists exemplify the profession in themselves. They are appropriately dressed, poised, well groomed, and take pride in practicing good nutrition. Their co-workers soon come to realize that home economists make rational consumer choices and control their time and money resources.

Because everyone lives in a home setting, including home economists, they are especially well equipped to empathize with their clients, patients, or students. Home economists understand the benefits that will be realized in the homes of those they serve. They evaluate the products and services of possible employers before they accept a position and satisfy themselves that clients will receive their money's worth. The home economists themselves evaluate their contribution to their employers and make sure the value of their production exceeds their pay.

ACHIEVING CERTIFICATION

The American Association of Family and Consumer Sciences (AAFCS) is the only national organization of family and consumer sciences, and it has a membership base of more than 14,500 members. These professionals include elementary, secondary, and postsecondary educators and administrators, cooperative extension educators, as well as dozens of other home economics professionals in government, business, and nonprofit entities.

In 1986, when the organization was still called the American Home Economics Association, the AAFCS established certification of home economics professionals. In the words of the AAFCS, becoming certified "is the most credible credential a family and consumer sciences professional can achieve."

The Certification Program of the AAFCS is designed to:

• promote continuing education and professional growth
• provide recognition to individuals

- increase employment opportunities
- foster excellence in the family and consumer sciences profession
- market the profession
- assist employers in recruitment and selection of highly qualified individuals within the profession

To achieve certification through the AAFCS, one must first have earned at least a bachelor's degree. The next step involves completing and passing the National Family and Consumer Sciences Examination. The AAFCS produces a study guide that explains what is included in the exam, provides a sample test, and also suggests additional readings and textbooks that can be consulted in preparation for the exam.

The actual exam covers three categories of family and consumer sciences. The first section treats family and consumer sciences as a profession, testing applicants on their knowledge of professional competencies and professional roles and responsibilities.

The second topic covers individuals, families, and the community. This section includes material on human development; the family as a system; interrelationships among individuals, family, and society; and an assessment of the effect that emerging issues will have on individuals and families.

Finally, the third area of the exam corresponds to professional specializations. This section tests the professional's knowledge of food, nutrition, and health; human development and family studies; textiles and apparel; housing, interiors, and design; family and consumer economics; hospitality management and food services; and family and consumer sciences, including education and/or communication.

ONGOING PROFESSIONAL DEVELOPMENT

A professional home economist's education continues even after one has passed the National Family and Consumer Sciences Examination. Every member must complete seventy-five Professional Development Units (PDUs) every three years in order to be recertified. These PDUs can be achieved by completing additional academic courses; participating in educational exhibits; attending professional meetings, in-service programs, and workshops; or researching and publishing articles related to the profession. Members are encouraged to design their own plans of study and accomplishment; there is a system for submitting the proposed PDU plans to the organization for prior approval.

CODE OF ETHICS

The American Association of Family and Consumer Sciences holds its members to a high level of ethical conduct.

The organization provides a set of ethical guidelines by which members can determine the propriety of their conduct.

According to the AAFCS:

> A member of the home economics profession and of the American Association of Family and Consumer Sciences shall:
>
> 1. Maintain the highest responsible standard of professional performance, upholding confidentiality and acting with intelligence, commitment, and enthusiasm.
> 2. Fulfill the obligation to continually upgrade and broaden personal professional competence.
> 3. Share professional competence with colleagues and clients, to enlarge and continue development of the profession.
> 4. Support the objectives of the American Association of Family and Consumer Sciences and contribute to its development through informed, active participation in its programs.
> 5. Advance public awareness and understanding of the profession.
> 6. Maintain a dedication of enhancing individual and family potential as a focus for professional efforts.

APPLYING FOR JOBS

The home economist starts a collection or portfolio of significant information about her or his work and experience before graduating. This would include summaries of research papers that were done at school, letters of recommendation from employers at part-time jobs, photographic copies of newspaper articles about the job, club notes, and letters including evidence of participation.

Examples of work completed may include lesson plans, newspaper stories, radio scripts, prepared brochures, trade journal articles, and reports of committee activities. All these serve to sell one's qualifications to prospective employers.

Before applying to a prospective employer, find out as much as possible about the organization so you can tailor your resume to their needs. Follow the recommendations given by standard resume forms in presenting your credentials. Obtain permission from those people you plan to include as references, making sure to include those who have had experience with your work. These may include teachers, employers, members of advisory councils, customers, co-workers, and officers of professional organizations. A letter of application that accompanies the resume should state your general career orientation and not be limited to a specific position.

When re-entering the profession after a period of full-time homemaking, account for nonpaid activity that illustrates your professional commitment, such as continuous participation in professional organizations, advisory councils, and boards of not-for-profit organizations. In applying for some positions it would be well to mention personal experiences that add to your competence, such as having remodeled your own home, designed costumes for a community theater, or having been a 4-H leader.

Whether it is your first position or a return to active employment, your college placement agency is a place to start looking for help. Let the counselors know about the locale in which you wish to work, and supply them with an updated list of your education and experience. Read the classified advertisements, and be sure to check those advertisements listed under "management" on the financial pages. Many home economists are qualified for these positions. Meet with professional employment agencies. Write or call the professional leaders in your field. You are the merchandiser of your profession.

PROFILE: STATE SENATOR

Jean was elected for another four-year term to the state senate last November. She had not thought of her home economics education and experience as preparation for politics but finds it is excellent.

She graduated with a degree in vocational home economics thirty years ago, was married the same summer, and has taught intermittently. She has four adult children and four grandchildren, a master's degree in adult education, and experience in vocational teaching, adult evening schools, and special classes for low-income students. She also has had some experience in assisting her husband, who is general manager of a wholesale corporation in the state's capital city. They live in an upper middle income area of the city where Jean has been active in AAUW, Rotary, parent-teacher groups, and religions organizations.

Jean decided to run for state government because of her own and several of her friends' and acquaintances' concern with the role the state government was taking in education, health, welfare, and family issues. She was particularly concerned about the arch-conservative attitude of the senator from their own district. Jean became convinced that she should run against that person.

Even though she was not experienced in politics, she and her supporters were gratified to find that many people agreed with their position, and Jean was able to win the election.

As a freshman senator she had a lot to learn about the ways of lobbyists, party caucuses, and political compromises. But her judgment was respected because of her knowledge of the lifestyles of lower, middle, and upper income families, their participation in community services, and the effect of the quality of those government services on the health, welfare, and education of families. Her schedule is arduous, especially during campaign time and during the legislative session. She has served on several task forces and committees appointed by the governor and the legislative leadership. She has introduced legislation to improve the situation of displaced homemakers by equalizing the ownership of marital property, providing more home health services, and reforming welfare regulations that encourage divorce and illegitimacy.

The salaries of state senator vary from state to state. In most states the senators do not vote to increase their own salaries, but they can vote to change the salaries of the next group of elected representatives. In other states, commissions are appointed to determine salary levels for government positions; some states require voter approval before raising the salaries of state officials.

In the late 1990s, salaries of lawmakers increased in a number of states. In California, lawmakers received a pay raise from $78,624 to $99,000, making California state senators the highest paid in the nation. New York state senators had gone without a pay raise since 1989; a 38 percent increase approved by the legislature in 1998 raised the pay to $79,500. At the other end of the range are senators in states such as Colorado and Arizona. In 1997 state senators received a 71 percent pay raise, raising their pay from a low of $17,500 to a still relatively low $30,000. And Arizona voters approved a 60 percent increase for their senators in 1999, bringing salaries from $15,000 to $24,000. The lowest salary for a state senator is in New Hampshire, where senators are paid only $100 a year, the privilege of representing their constituency serving as reward enough. By contrast, members of the United States Congress earned $136,700 in 1999.

The challenge of making her state into one with an environment conducive to the development of children and the welfare of families is enough to keep Jean working as hard as she now does as a senator for several more sessions.

SUGGESTED ADDITIONAL READING

Hitch, Elizabeth J. and June Pierce Youatt. *Communicating Family and Consumer Sciences: A Guidebook for Professionals.* Tinley Park, IL: Goodheart-Willcox Co., 1995.

CONCLUSION: THE ROLE OF THE HOME ECONOMIST IN THE TWENTY-FIRST CENTURY

As we enter the twenty-first century, the role of the home economist becomes one of increasing importance. By the 1990s, public discourse focused intently on issues related to parenting, child welfare, and the social and vocational skills of young adults. Incidents of school and workplace violence dramatically highlighted the need for strong moral guidance and compassionate counseling. Special attention began to be focused on children in at-risk populations, such as inner-city minorities and rural youths in economically depressed regions. Similarly, professionals refocused their efforts to reach parents and assist them in their important task of guiding their youngsters toward fulfilling futures. The concensus arose that the goal of building healthy family relationships not only affected the child in question, but the society at large.

Another trend in society concerns senior citizens. Organizations such as the American Association of Family and

Consumer Sciences have strengthened their efforts to promote research and education that will improve the lives of the elderly population. One aspect of these efforts is exploring the ways that intergenerational relationships enhance the mental, emotional, and physical well-being of older Americans. Not incidentally, these same intergenerational activities, such as community events that bring senior citizens and teens together, also have a positive effect on the younger generation, providing many youngsters with a sense of continuity and community.

Advances in communications and technologies provide an opportunity for greater involvement on the part of the home economics professional. These new developments bridge distances, bring up-to-date knowledge into the home, and facilitate greater communication.

As you consider your options in this extraordinarily active and responsive field, one final word of advice: keep learning.

Broaden your horizons, seek out new experiences, keep your eyes and ears open, and maintain an open heart.

Home economics is a powerful and unique career direction. It brings you into the homes of neighbors and complete strangers, into communities that will feel very familiar to you, as well as worlds that will be completely foreign. You might be working in another corner of the globe; or you might be involved with a child care center right down the street.

Wherever it takes you, be certain that you have chosen a field that provides you with unparalleled opportunities to truly assist others in their efforts to find more happiness and balance in their lives. Your energy, commitment, and expertise are needed as we enter the next century; they will serve as beacons of light.

ASSOCIATIONS

The following list includes several of the organizations related to the profession of home economics. If you have access to the Internet, either through a home computer, college, or public library, you can find out a great deal by visiting these organizations' web pages. Alternately, you can write to them to request more information on membership and educational opportunities.

American Association of Family and Consumer Sciences
   1555 King Street
   Alexandria, VA 22314
   Internet address: www.aafcs.org

American Association of Marriage and Family Therapy
   1133 Fifteenth Street, NW
   Suite 300
   Washington, DC 20005
   Internet address: www.aamft.org

The American Association of Retired Persons
   601 E Street NW
   Washington, DC 20049
   Internet address: www.aarp.org

The American Association of Textile Chemists and Colorists
    One Davis Drive, P. O. Box 12215
    Research Triangle Park, NC 27709-2215
    Internet address: www.aatcc.org

American Council on Consumer Interests
    240 Stanley Hall
    University of Missouri
    Columbia, MO 65211
    Internet address: www.acci.ps.missouri.edu

American Counseling Association
    5999 Stevenson Avenue
    Alexandria, VA 22304

American Dietetic Association
    216 West Jackson Boulevard
    Chicago, IL 60606-6995
    Internet address: www.eatright.org

American Society for Interior Designers
    608 Massachusetts Avenue NE
    Washington, DC 20002-6006
    Internet address: www.asid.org

The American Vocational Association
    1410 King Street
    Alexandria, VA 22314
    Internet address: www.avaonline.org

Association for Childhood Education International
    11501 Georgia Avenue, Suite 315
    Wheaton, MD 20902-1924

Council for Early Childhood Professional Recognition
    2460 Sixteenth Street NW
    Washington, DC 20009

Council on Hotel, Restaurant, and Institutional Education
    1200 Seventeenth Street NW
    Washington, DC 20036-3097

Families and Work Institute
330 Seventh Avenue
New York, NY 10001
Internet address: www.familiesandworkinst.org

Family Education Network
20 Park Plaza, Suite 1215
Boston, MA 02116
Internet address: www.familyeducation.com

Family Resource Coalition of America
20 North Wacker Drive, Suite 1100
Chicago, IL 60606
Internet address: www.frca.org

Fashion Group International
597 Fifth Avenue, 8th Floor
New York, NY 10017
Internet address: www.fga.org

Foundation for Interior Design Education Research
60 Monroe Center NW
Grand Rapids, MI 49305
Internet address: www.fider.org

Industrial Designers Society of America
1142-E Walker Road
Great Falls, VA 22066
Internet address: www.idsa.org

International Association of Financial Planning
Suite B-300
5775 Glenridge Drive NE
Atlanta, GA 30328-5364
Internet address: www.iafp.org

International Executive Housekeepers Association, Inc.
1001 Eastwind Drive, Suite 301
Westerville, OH 43081-3361
Internet address: www.ieha.org

National Association for the Education of Young Children
  1509 Sixteenth Street NW
  Washington, DC 20036

National Association of Health Career Schools
  750 First Street NW, Suite 940
  Washington, DC 20002-4241

National Association for Home Care
  228 Seventh Street SE
  Washington, DC 20003

National Association of Social Workers
  750 First Street NE, Suite 700
  Washington, DC 20002-4241
  Internet address: www.naswdc.org

National Council on Family Relations
  3989 Central Avenue NE, Suite 550
  Minneapolis, MN 55421
  Internet address: www.ncfr.com

National Foundation for Consumer Credit
  8611 Second Avenue, Suite 100
  Silver Spring, MD 20910
  Internet address: www.nfcc.org

National Restaurant Association
  1200 Seventeenth Street NW
  Washington, DC 20036-30970

Peace Corps
  1111 Twentieth Street NW
  Washington, DC 20526
  Internet address: www.peacecorps.gov

UNIVERSITIES AND COLLEGES

The following programs of professional study have been accredited by the American Association for Family and Consumer Sciences (formerly the American Home Economics Association). In order for a program to receive accreditation, it must meet or exceed certain nationally established criteria and hold membership in AAFCS's Higher Education Unit. The accreditation process assures that graduates of these programs have had formal preparation that meets the AAFCS's standards.

University of Akron, School of Family & Consumer Sciences

University of Alabama, College of Human Environmental Sciences

Alcorn State University, Department of Family & Consumer Sciences

Appalachian State University, Department of Family & Consumer Sciences

University of Arkansas—Fayetteville, School of Human Environmental Sciences

University of Arkansas—Pine Bluff, Department of Human Sciences

Auburn University, School of Human Sciences

Baylor University, Department of Family & Consumer Sciences

California State University—Long Beach, Department of Family & Consumer Sciences *

California State University—Northridge, Department of Family Environmental Sciences

Carson Newman College, Division of Family & Consumer Sciences

CUNY—Queens College, Department of Family Nutrition & Exercise Science

Delta State University, Division of Family & Consumer Sciences

Eastern Illinois University, School of Family & Consumer Sciences

Florida State University, College of Human Sciences

Fort Valley State University, Department of Family & Consumer Sciences

Framingham State College, Department of Family & Consumer Sciences

University of Georgia, College of Family & Consumer Sciences

Illinois State University, Department of Family & Consumer Sciences

Indiana State University, Department of Family & Consumer Sciences

Iowa State University, College of Family & Consumer Sciences

University of Kentucky, College of Human Environmental Sciences

Louisiana State University, School of Human Ecology

Louisiana Tech University, School of Human Ecology

McNesse State University, Department of Family & Consumer Sciences

University of Memphis, Department of Consumer Science & Education

Middle Tennessee State University, Department of Human Sciences

University of Mississippi, Department of Family & Consumer Sciences

Mississippi State University, School of Human Sciences

Montana State University, Family & Consumer Sciences

Montclair State University, Department of Human Ecology

University of Montevallo, Department of Family & Consumer Sciences

University of Nebraska—Lincoln, College of Human Resources & Family Sciences

Nicholls State University, Department of Family & Consumer Sciences

North Carolina A&T State, Department of Human Environment & Family Sciences

Northeast Louisiana State University, Department of Family & Consumer Sciences*

Northwest Missouri State University, Department of Human Environmental Sciences

Northwestern State University of Louisiana, Department of Family & Consumer Sciences

Ohio University, School of Human & Consumer Sciences

Oklahoma State University, College of Human Environmental Sciences

Oregon State University, College of Home Economics & Education

San Francisco State University, Department of Consumer & Family Studies/Dietetics

South Carolina State University, Department of Family & Consumer Sciences

South Dakota State University, College of Family & Consumer Sciences

University of Southern Mississippi, School of Family & Consumer Sciences

Southern University & A&M, Division of Family & Consumer Sciences

Southwest Missouri State University, Department of Consumer & Family Studies

Southwest Texas State University, Department of Family & Consumer Sciences

University of Southwestern Louisiana, School of Human Resources

Stephen F. Austin State University, Department of Human Sciences

SUNY College at Oneonta, Department of Human Ecology

University of Tennessee—Knoxville, College of Human Ecology

University of Tennessee—Martin, Department of Human Environmental Sciences

Tennessee State University, Department of Family & Consumer Sciences

Texas Tech University, College of Human Sciences

Utah State University, College of Family Life

Virginia Polytechnic Institute and State University, College of Human Resources & Education

Western Carolina University, Department of Human Environmental Sciences

*Provisional accreditation as of May, 1999.

SAMPLE COURSES OF STUDY: HOME ECONOMICS EDUCATION

The requirements for becoming certified to teach home economics will vary from program to program and from state to state. Every university and college has different "core" classes—the classes one must take in order to receive a bachelor of science degree in home economics (or family and consumer sciences). This invariably means fulfilling the core requirements of the school, such as class work in English, history, languages, and mathematics, as well as meeting the specific requirements of your department.

Depending on your area of specialization, you also will probably have to take classes in related departments; for example, some schools combine the home economics communication degree with course work from the university's journalism program.

To qualify as a home economics teacher, you will study the core topics related to the field. At most schools you also will have to complete course work in the college or university's teachers college or other program that prepares educators.

Here we present two sample curricula that will give you a general idea of how one prepares to become a home economics teacher. Make sure you check with the colleges and universities where you apply to make sure that you understand their particular requirements.

Example One: Major in Home Economics Education (with optional special education classes)

Basic Courses:

Individual and Family Development
Management for Modern Living
Foundations of Expression in Home Economics
Research in Home Economics Topics
Field Study in Guided Home Economics Project

Sample Specialized Courses:

Introduction to Textiles
Apparel Construction
History of Textiles and Apparel
Apparel and Human Behavior
Introduction to Food Science
Nutrition for Life
Cultural Aspects of Food and Nutrition
Nutrition for Mothers and Children
Introduction to Human Habitats
Contemporary Issues in Housing
Consumer Issues and Problems

Introduction to Family Finance
Marriage and Family Relations
Child Growth and Development
Early Childhood Education

Example Two: Degree in Home Economics Education (with greater number of required courses)

Some programs will have a larger number of classes that the school considers *required* courses for home economics education majors. For example, the following curriculum consists entirely of required classes, which would be supplemented by course work in the education department as well as extensive fieldwork and a student teaching internship.

Requirements for a Major in Home Economics Education:

Foods I and II
Clothing I and II
Nutrition and Health
Nutrition and the Life Cycle
Art in the Home
Family Resource Management
Housing and Equipment
Advanced Food Science
Advanced Clothing
Human Anatomy and Physiology
Microbiology
Chemistry of Life

Chemical Principles
Models of Behaviorism
Models of Information Processing
Models of Personal and Social Growth
Curriculum Development in Secondary School Subject
    Area (Home Economics)
Professional Semester (Student Teaching)
Psychology of Exceptional Children

These courses may be supplemented by additional work in psychology, nutrition, family financial management, or another home economics–related area.